THE DIAMOND SUTRA

THE DIAMOND SUTRA
(CHIN-KANG-CHING)

OR

PRAJNA-PARAMITA

TRANSLATED FROM THE CHINESE
WITH AN INTRODUCTION AND NOTES
BY
WILLIAM GEMMELL

FIRST PUBLISHED BY
KEGAN PAUL, TRENCH, TURNER & CO.,
LTD
BROADWAY HOUSE, 68-74 CARTER LANE, E.C.
LONDON, 1912

William Gemmell (pictured centre, about 1893) with his ordained Buddhist mentors; Chang-Ming the chief monk (Seng-Kwan) of the Chen-Chou prefecture in Hu-Nan, and Chich-Hsien, his aged and affectionate teacher.

THIS EDITION
IS RESPECTFULLY REPRODUCED BY
THE ORIGINAL AUTHOR'S GRANDSON
OF THE SAME NAME

WILLIAM GEMMELL

2022

ROAD TO OBI, PO BOX 58,
MAPLETON, QUEENSLAND 4560 AUSTRALIA

ISBN: 978-0-646-96083-8

PUBLISHER'S NOTE

The Diamond Sutra is considered a most significant contributor to the Mahayana Buddhist tradition, being an extensive discourse between the Buddha and a senior disciple, Subhuti. The date of the original Sutra's Sanskrit composition is lost in time, but the earliest Chinese translations, upon which this interpretation is based, date from the early 5th Century.

William Gemmell, the interpreter and original author of this work, was just twenty-one years of age in 1890 when he left his Scottish home and took up residence in a Buddhist temple in Hunan, China. For most of the following decade he pursued a Chinese classical education under his Buddhist teachers, until 1900, when the 'Boxer Rebellion' provided a catalyst for a brief return to Scotland. After a year's absence, he returned to China a newly married man and took up residence in Hubei as a professional scholar, interpreter, teacher and advisor. He eventually returned to Scotland in 1910, along with his Scottish bride and their young family. He died in 1947.

In this modern re-publication of William's work, no attempt has been made to either revise his interpretation of Buddhist doctrine, or any other doctrine, or to modernise his language and anglicisation of Chinese terms, names and phrases. Indeed, particular effort has been made to preserve the original publication's context, look and feel, given the original's 1912 publication date, and that the author was originally the product of a Victorian-era Scottish and strictly Christian education.

ROAD TO OBI
Australia, April 2022

FOREWORD

I feel somewhat embarrassed to admit I was past sixty years old before I was inspired to properly examine and thereby gain a respectful awareness of our grandfather WG's scholarship, and his Herculean effort, in rendering from Chinese and endeavouring to explain, both in English and in a contemporary European context (the year the RMS Titanic sank, 1912), his interpretation of *The Diamond Sutra*, considered by many the most powerful and influential of the Mahayana Buddhist texts.

WG's publication was one of the earliest of this important Sutra into the English language. In his following Preface he tells us his intention was not to compete with earlier and perhaps more pedagogical translations, from Sanskrit by Max Müller and from Chinese by Samuel Beal, but rather to fulfil the more workaday purpose of making these important Buddhist teachings available, in the English language, to a general European or Western readership. In his quaintly Victorian style, WG explains:

"It would appear that the peculiar charm of the Buddhist philosophy, and the remarkable purity of the Buddhist faith, are becoming more generally appreciated in Europe. Should this imperfect rendering of The Diamond Sutra, even in the faintest degree, confirm a just sense of appreciation, or prove a gentle incentive for further enquiry, then its unexpected publication may prove to be not entirely unjustified."

Those who may be inclined to mount a scholarly criticism or even denigration of WG's work, including those elucidated in his Introduction and its accompanying Footnotes, should perhaps seek to find within themselves a sympathetic appreciation of the context in which WG's publication was made. The place was London England

and the year 1912; the Buddha's teachings were almost entirely unexamined in the West; the European mindset he hoped to penetrate was overwhelmingly Christian; and the whole region was soon to be distracted by the calamatous 1914-18 "War to End All Wars."

From a commercial perspective, WG's timing might be said to have been problematic, at best. From a Buddhist viewpoint however, his work of a lifetime might have been expected to transcend generations. Indeed, WG would doubtless be most gratified to learn that today, and throughout the West, Buddhist practice is thoroughly entrenched and continues to expand, engaging not only many adherents of European ancestry, but also millions of globally emigrant Buddhists from many Asian countries.

In this context also, and perhaps not too surprisingly to more enlightened Buddhists, the date of my own birth coincided with WG's death in November 1947. On that basis, I trust that my rediscovery and republication of his work will serve as both celebration and extension of his most worthy 'life's purpose' — the continuing promotion of the *"charm of the Buddhist philosophy, and the remarkable purity of the Buddhist faith."*

WILLIAM GEMMELL
The Author's Grandson
Australia, April 2022

PREFACE

This English version of *The Diamond Sutra*,[1] translated from the Chinese text of Kumarajiva, owes its inception to successive conversations with a friend, profoundly interested in interpreting oriental systems of philosophy.

During these conversations, renderings into English were made of numerous passages from the works of Confucius, Mencius and Lao-Tsz.

Having briefly surveyed these fertile fields of thought, we passed by natural progression into the delectable Buddhist realm. Some passages from the *Chinese Sutras*, comprising text and annotations, were consecutively examined, and variously considered. Eventually it was suggested that *The Diamond Sutra*, perhaps one of the most metaphysical of the works ascribed to Buddha, be conveniently rendered into the English language.

In order that the rather unfamiliar text might assume due intelligibility, parallel passages and annotations were subjoined, as the pleasant work of translating proceeded. The idea of printing and publishing the resulting text seemed to follow as a natural sequence.

Already there do exist other renderings of *The Diamond Sutra* in the English language, from the Sanskrit by Max Müller and from the Chinese by Samuel Beal. This new version does not seek to enter into rivalry with these erudite works; and a possible apology which might be

---

1 A learned Chinese commentator thus explained the Sutra's rather striking title: "As the diamond exceeds all other precious gems in brilliance and indestructibility; so, also, does the wisdom of The Diamond Sutra transcend, and shall outlive, all other knowledge known to philosophy."

readily offered for the publication of this modest volume is, that the scholarly productions of Müller and Beal, in their present forms, are perhaps somewhat inaccessible to the general English language reader.

It would appear that the peculiar charm of the Buddhist philosophy, and the remarkable purity of the Buddhist faith, are becoming more generally appreciated in Europe. Should this imperfect rendering of *The Diamond Sutra,* even in the faintest degree, confirm this just sense of appreciation, and prove a gentle incentive for further enquiry, then its unexpected publication may prove to be not entirely unjustified.

In recording our many obligations to those scholars whose works were frequently consulted, we also give expression to a hope that nothing of importance is omitted which ought to be gratefully acknowledged.

It may also be permissible to express admiration of the piety, and appreciation of the friendship, of those learned monks in Central China, to whom we are everlastingly indebted, for even a slight initiation into those inexhaustible truths which are alike the heritage, and the glory, of the discipline of Buddha. Among these we should like to specify are Chang-Ming, the chief monk (Seng-Kwan) of Chen-Chou prefecture, Hu-Nan, and the aged and affectionate Chich-Hsien.

WM. GEMMELL
Pollockshields, Glasgow
6th September, 1912

INTRODUCTION

The Diamond Sutra is one of the most valued and widely read philosophical works in Buddhist literature. It is very popular amongst ardent Buddhists in China, and excepting the *Lotus of the Good Law*, and the *Long-Yen-Ching*,[1] perhaps no other Sutra ascribed to Buddha is regarded in China with so great esteem.

In Japan, *The Diamond Sutra* appears to be perused extensively by what Max Müller[2] termed the Shin-Gon sect, founded by Ko-Bo, a disciple of the renowned pilgrim Hiuen-Tsang, in about the year 816 A.D.

The Diamond Sutra was written originally in Sanskrit, and in process of time translated into Tibetan, Chinese, Mongol and Manchu languages. It represents the Mahayana school of Buddhist thought[3], which flourished primarily at Tchakuka, and thereafter influenced appreciably a considerable part of the Buddhist faith.

In the year 1836 Sándor Kőrösi Csoma published an account of the Tibetan translation, which interesting

---

1 "The Sutra of firm establishment in all doctrine, describing clearly the secret merit and attainments in the religious life of Tathāgata" (Compare Edkins' *Chinese Buddhism*) See also the preface to *The Vagrakkhedika* (The Diamond Cutter -Ed)

2 See preface to *The Vagrakkhedika*

3 The Mahāyāna tradition is the largest of Buddhism's major traditions. Among the earliest and most important references to the term are those that occur in the Lotus Sūtra (Sanskrit Saddharma Pundarīka Sūtra) dating between the 1st century BCE and the 1st century CE. The term Mahāyāna meaning "Great Vehicle" was originally an honorary synonym for Bodhisattvayāna ("Bodhisattva Vehicle"), the vehicle of a bodhisattva seeking buddhahood for the benefit of all sentient beings. The term Mahāyāna was therefore formed independently at an early date as a synonym for the path and the teachings of the Bodhisattvas.

document may be consulted in Vol. XX of the *Asiatic Researches*. The Diamond Sutra is therein designated "the Sutra of Wonderful Effects," a treatise by means of which Sakyamuni Buddha[1] instructs Subhuti, one of his conspicuous disciples, in the Prajna-Paramita of transcendent wisdom.[2]

To Kumarajiva,[3] a native of Kashmir, who gained distinction as a monk of the later Qin dynasty[4] (A.D. 384-417), is conceded the honour of having first translated *The Diamond Sutra* into the Chinese language. Of subsequent Chinese translations, perhaps the most noteworthy is the text ascribed to the scholar Xuan Zang, completed about the middle of the seventh century.[5]

A rendering into English of Kumarajiva's Chinese translation was accomplished by the Rev. S. Beal, and published in *The Journal of Royal Asiatic Society*, 1864-65. The text and German translation of the Tibetan

---

1 The ancient ascetic sage (born approx 500 B.C.) on whose teachings Buddhism is founded and in this interpretation is referred to as "Sakyamuni Buddha," is today variously known as Gautama Buddha, Siddhārtha Gautama, Shakyamuni Buddha, or simply the Buddha, after the title of Buddha.

2 See the preface to Max Müller's *The Vagrakkhadika*.

3 Kumarajiva was referred to as "one of four suns of Buddhism" (Tchatvara Suryas). He laboured in China as a most active and judicious translator, and is credited for having introduced a new alphabet. One of Kumarajiva's Chinese designations — *Tung-Sheo* – meant that, although he was young in years, he was ripe in the wisdom and virtues of old age. (Compare Eitel's *Handbook of Chinese Buddhism*.)

4 Beal stated in his preface to the *Kin-King-King*, that "it was translated first into the Chinese by Kumara-Jiva (A.D. 405), who was brought into China from Thibet (Tibet)."

5 Other translations, worthy of recognition, are those attributed respectively to Bodhiruki, (A.D. 509), Paramartha (A.D. 562), Dharmagupa, of the Sui dynasty (A.D. 589-618), and I-Tsing (A.D. 703). (Compare the preface in *The Vagrakkhadika*.)

INTRODUCTION　　　　　　　　　xiii

version was published in 1873 by M. Schmidt, in the *Memoires de l'Acadenie St Petersbourg*. The Mongolian translation was presented by the Baron de Costada to the library of the Institut de France. The Manchu translation is in the possession of M. de Harles, who, with the aid of the Tibetan, Manchu and Chinese versions, published a French translation of the Sanskrit text of *The Diamond Sutra* in the *Journal Asiatique*,[1] 1892. It has been observed[2] that "at first sight it may seem as if this metaphysical treatise hardly deserve the world-wide-reputation which it has attained." Regarding this descriptive "world-wide reputation, devout Buddhists might suggest in extenuating, that throughout many centuries, the "spiritual wisdom" of *The Diamond Sutra* produced in countless minds a "conscious blessedness of perfect peace". This "spiritual wisdom" also appeared to be a "strong incentive to holiness" and a grateful inspiration to those who had attained "the path which leads to Nirvana". In a few renowned temples of Central China, our Buddhist friends frequently affirmed that, by contemplating the "spiritual wisdom" of *The Diamond Sutra*, the mind would inevitably become "transfused with the mellow light of imperishable truth."

In the preface to *The Vagrakkhadika*, Max Müller made a critical observation regarding certain peculiarities of "style adopted in this treatise by the Buddhist philosophers who wanted to convince their hearers of the truth of their philosophy." From the Sanskrit text, perhaps it is difficult to realise fully what Asvaghocha[3] described as

---

1 This information may be found in Max Müller's *Vagrakkhadika* which, when written, represented a considerable part of the Western knowledge available on he subject.

2 By Max Müller.

3 The Chinese *Ma-Ming*.

the "persuasiveness of Buddha's eloquence;"[1] yet we may quite appreciate the academic instinct of Kumarajiva, whose work on *The Diamond Sutra* bears evidence of a laudable endeavour to create a classic, which in the Chinese language is considered almost entirely beyond reproach.

In all our aspirations to translate and interpret Buddhist texts, perhaps it might prove advantageous to bear in mind the significant words incorporated in *The Light of Asia* —

> "And time hath blurred their script and ancient sense.
> Which once was new and mighty, moving all."

Max Müller stated that *The Diamond Sutra* represents a treatise on "metaphysical agnosticism," and he excuses its "endless repetition of the same process of reasoning" on the assumption that the subject matter of the *Sutra* is "probably perfectly familiar to children and ignorant persons".

By referring to our Chinese texts, we are led to suppose that *The Diamond Sutra* was "delivered expressly for those who had entered the Path which leads to Nirvana," and for those who are "attaining to the ultimate plane of Buddhic thought." Our Chinese annotations also appear to be unanimous in suggesting that the "spiritual wisdom" of *The Diamond Sutra* is understood only in its rudimentary forms, by those of immature or uninitiated mind.

Concerning what has been termed the "agnosticism" of The Diamond Sutra, Sakyamuni Buddha, when he admissibly delivered the text, indicated clearly that there is a sense in which the "highest perfect knowledge"[2] may

---

1 Compare the Chinese text *Chi-Sin-Pien* — *The Awakening of Faith*.

2 In the preface to *The Vagrakkhadika*.

INTRODUCTION

be referred to as "unknown." Dante appears to have had a similar difficulty regarding "knowledge" and "power"[1] wherewith to express the higher form of spiritual experience; and the following lines, constituting the opening stanzas of his *Paradiso*, may serve to elucidate the Buddhist position, and make it perhaps more intelligible to those who are as yet unfamiliar with its particular modes of thought: —

> *"La gloria di colui che tutto move*
> *Per l'universo penetra, e risplende*
> *In una parte più, a meno altrove.*
> *"Nel ciel che più de la sua luce prende*
> *Fu' io, e vidi cose che ridere*
> *Nè sa nè può qual di la sù discende . . .*
> *"Perchè, appressando sè al suo disire,*
> *Nostro intelletto[2] si profonda tanto,*
> *Che dietro la memoria non può ire."*[3]

In order to fully appreciate the philosophy of *The Diamond Sutra*, it is necessary to correctly interpret the

---

[1] "Supreme Spiritual Wisdom". In Beal's *Kin-Kong-King*, "The unsurpassed, just and enlightened heart." Sanskrit, *Annuttara Samyak Sambodhi Hridaya*.

[2] According to the text of *The Diamond Sutra*, the intellect of Sakyamuni Buddha sank so profoundly into the past that he was enabled to speak confidently of his experiences in previous incarnations.

[3] *"The glory of the one who moves all things*
permeates the universe and glows
in one part more and in another less.
"I was within the heaven that receives
more of His light; and I saw things that he
who from that height descends, forgets or cannot speak . . .
"For nearing its desired end,
our intellect sinks into an abyss
so deep that memory fails to follow it."

meaning of the Buddhist terminology. In this connection, the Sanskrit *Dharma* — usually rendered into Chinese by "*Fah*" and English by "*Law*"— appears to merit our immediate attention,

Max Müller, with his ample knowledge, stated that *Dharma*, "in the ordinary Buddhist phraseology, may be correctly rendered as *Law*; thus the whole teaching of Buddha is named *Saddharma* —'The Good Law.'

"What *The Diamond Sutra* aims to teach is that all objects, differing from one another by their Dharmas, are illusive, or as we should say, phenomenal and subjective, that they are, in fact, of our own making; the products of our own mind." With those noteworthy observations, there is embodied in the preface to *The Vagrakkhadika*, the following interesting suggestion, that the Greek εἶδος — whatever is seen, form, shape, figure —appears to be the equivalent of the Sanskrit Dharma.

Spence Hardy, a distinguished writer on Buddhism, made a suggestion of perhaps equal importance, with reference to the correct interpretation of Dharma. In the well-known volume *Eastern Monachism*, there occurs the following relevant passage: "The second of the three great treasures is called *Dhammo*, or in Sinhalese, *Dharmma*. This word has various meanings, but it is here to be understood in the sense of *truth*."

Rhys Davids in his useful volume Buddhism, indicated that "Dharma (Pali *Dhamma*) is not Law, but that which underlies and includes the Law—a word often most difficult to understand and translate, but best rendered here by Truth and Righteousness." [1]

---

[1] Dr Edkins, in his scholarly work *Chinese Buddhism*, seems to have regarded "the Law or body of doctrine" as an accurate definition of Dharma.

Dr Eitel, in his *Handbook of Chinese Buddhism*, explained Dharma by "Fah" — "Law" and observed that it is "a general

INTRODUCTION xvii

Perhaps it may be opportune to remark, that had Kumarajiva regarded "form," "truth," or "righteousness," as expressing adequately the Sanskrit Dharma, those familiar terms being obviously at his command, might have been utilised at pleasure. Like the cultured Asvaghocha, Kumarakiva may have regarded the "nature" of the Law as "co-extensive with the illimitable ocean of being,"[1] and within that ample compass, perhaps he thought there might synthetically be included those beautifuly-defined concepts, "form," "truth," and "righteousness."

Chinese annotators of *The Diamond Sutra* seldom adversely criticise its classic terminology, or suggest many inapplicable alternative renderings. They appear to have surveyed the realm of "spiritual wisdom" enunciated by Shakyamuni Buddha, and thereafter to have become greatly impressed by the thought that, in its Essence, it might possibly be inexhaustible. This may partly explain their motive for incorporating in the commentary a familiar passage from Lao Zi[2], "Infinite truth is inexpressible"[3] — which in a measure illustrates the appreciable difficulty of stating, in exact terms of philosophy, the equivalent of the Buddhist "Law".

---

term for religious objects, especially for the Buddhist Canon."

Smith, in *Asoka, Buddhist Emperor of India*, suggested that the Chinese "*Hsiao*" (piety), and Latin "*pietas*," coincide with the Sanskrit term Dharma.

1 The Chinese phrase is "Fah-sing-chen-ru-hai."

2 Chinese: Lǎozī (lit. "Old Master"), also Lao-Tzu or Lao-Tze, was an ancient Chinese philosopher and writer. He is known as the reputed author of the Tao Te Ching and the founder of philosophical Taoism, and as a deity in religious Taoism and traditional Chinese religions.

3 See the *Tao-Teh-Ching*. Compare, also, the statement attributed to Confucius — "Nature and Truth cannot be adequately expressed."

In our intercourse with Buddhist monks, we heard the rather engaging suggestion that the familiar Christian phrase, "the law of the spirit of life," contains a spiritual concept which appears to closely approximate the idea of the "Law" of Buddha. Those monks seemed to believe that the "Law" (or Dharma) enters quietly and operates imperceptibly within every natural and spiritual sphere; and that they have at least a semblance of reason for their belief, the following lines clearly indicate: —

"This is its touch upon the blossomed rose,
The fashion in its hand shaped lotus leaves.

"That is its painting on the glorious clouds,
And these its emeralds on the peacock's train.

"Out of the dark it wrought the heart of man,
Out of dull shells the pheasant's pencilled neck.

"It spreadeth forth for flight the eagle's wings
What time she beareth home her prey.

"This is its work upon the things ye see
The unseen things are more; men's hearts and minds,
The thoughts of peoples and their ways and wills,
Those, too, the great Law binds."[1]

As we consider the manifold operations of this "Law which moves to righteousness," perhaps we may gradually appreciate the dignified mind of Sakyamuni, when he addressed Subhuti, saying: "What is usually referred to as the 'Law' of Buddha, is not in reality a 'Law' attributive to

---

1 Compare *The Light of Asia*. Perhaps this aspect of the "Law" of Buddha may be conceived of as harmonising with Shakespeare's idea of a "Divinity".

INTRODUCTION

Buddha, it is merely termed the 'Law' of Buddha."[1]

The Sanskrit term "Samgna",[2] usually rendered into Chinese by "Ming," and into English by "Name," seems to deserve further attention. Like the term Dharma, a clear knowledge of "Samgna" is indispensable for a true understanding of our text.

In one of the opening passages of *The Diamond Sutra* we find that Sakyamuni Buddha, in reply to an enquiry by Subhuti, suggests that by means of this "wisdom," enlightened disciples are enabled to bring into subjection "every inordinate desire."

"Every species of life, whether hatched in the egg, formed in the womb, produced by metamorphosis, with or without form or intelligence, possessing or devoid of natural instinct

---

1 It may be interesting to observe that, according to our Chinese text, Sakyamuni Buddha evidently disclaimed any desire to either formulate or perpetuate a stereotyped system of "Law" or "doctrine." Sakyamuni Buddha also made it plain, that the "Law" which he enunciated, was presented before the minds of his disciples in the simile of a "raft" — a thing to be abandoned when the mind "touched the further shore" of everlasting truth. It seems to be in this tentative sense that intellectual Buddhists regard all ecclesiastical institutions, priesthoods, dogmas, ordinances, etc.; and we have met monks who would classify "belief" in the "efficacy" of religious rites or ceremonies, with obnoxious forms of "heresy" and "immorality." (Compare Rhys Davids' *Buddhism*.) With regard to the Buddhist objection concerning the "efficacy" of "religious rites," compare the noble sentiments expressed in the following lines, delightfully rendered by Sir Edwin Arnold from the *Bhagavad-Gita (The Song Celestial)*: —
"Serenity of soul, benignity,
Sway of the silent spirit, constant stress
To sanctify the nature, — these things make
Good rite, and true religiousness of mind."
2 Max Müller suggests that Samgna and Dharma "correspond in many respects to the "Vedantica Namarupe" — in Chinese Ming-Seh — name, form, or characteristic".

— from these changeful conditions of being I command you to seek deliverance in the transcendental concepts of Nirvana. Thus you shall obtain deliverance from the idea of an immeasurable, innumerable, and illimitable world of sentient life; but, in reality there is no idea of a world of sentient life from which to obtain deliverance. And why? Because, in the mind of an enlightened disciple, there have ceased to exist such arbitrary ideas of phenomena as an entity, a being, a living being, or a personality."

A similar process of reasoning appears to permeate the whole of *The Diamond Sutra*, and whether appertaining to a living being, a virtue, a condition of mind, a Buddhist pure land[1], or a personal Buddha, there is implied in each concept a spiritual essence, only imperfectly described, if not entirely overlooked, in the ordinary use of each particular name. Shakespeare enquired, "What's in a name?" And in a thought inspired by a rose and its delicious fragrance, suggested, with Buddha, that there is little, or nothing in a name, which explains the real nature of an object. Even a "particle of dust" seems, to the Buddhist mind, to embody in its composition a subtle spiritual element, entirely "inscrutable" and quite "incomprehensible."

According to the Mahayana School of Buddhist thought, objects and their respective names are both unreal and illusory. Objects and names in the abstract represent merely the products of untutored and unenlightened minds. All things appear to be subject to the irrevocable Laws of change and decay, so that nothing is real in the sense that it is permanent. As the things we see are temporal, it is essential for our intellectual development that we focus upon spiritual matters which are Unseen and Eternal. Many minds are susceptible of

---

1 In Mahayana Buddhism, Pure Land is the celestial realm, or pure abode, of a Buddha or Bodhisattva.

INTRODUCTION xxi

deception by the fleeting phenomenon of life; but behind these phenomena there is an essential element, entirely spiritual,[1] uninfluenced by arbitrary ideas or changeful conditions, which "pervades all things," and is "pure" and "everlasting".

The following interesting outline of Mahayana doctrine[2] was prepared by Mr. S. Kuroda, approved by several influential Buddhist communions in Japan, and "published with authority at Tokyo in 1893":—

"All things that are produced by causes and conditions are inevitably destined to extinction. There is nothing that has any reality; when conditions begin, things begin to appear, when conditions cease, these things likewise cease to exist. Like the foam in the water, like the lightning[3] flash, and like the floating, swiftly vanishing clouds, they are only of momentary duration. As all things have no permanent nature of their own, so there is no actuality in pure and impure, rough and fine, large and small, far and near, knowable and unknowable, etc. On this account it is sometimes said that all things are nothing. The apparent phenomena around us, however, are produced by mental operations within us, and thus distinctions are established...

"All things are included under subject and object. The subject is an entity in which mental operations are awakened whenever there are objects, while the object consists of all things, visible and invisible, knowable and unknowable, etc. The subject is not something that occupies some space in the body alone, nor does object exist outside of the subject...[4]

---

1 Some Japanese Buddhists appear to regard this purely spiritual element as "essence of mind".
2 From the preface to *The Vagrakkhedika*
3 Compare page 74 footnote 1, *Kin-Kong-King*
4 Compare the interesting dialogue *The Enlightenment of*

INTRODUCTION

"The various phenomena which appear as subjects and objects are divided into two kinds; the perceptible and knowable, the imperceptible and unknowable. . . Now, what are the imperceptible and unknowable phenomena?

"Through the influence of habitual delusions, boundless worlds, innumerable varieties of things spring up in the mind. This boundless universe and these subtle ideas are not perceptible and knowable; only Bodhisattvas[1] believe, understand and become perfectly convinced of these through the contemplation of Vidyamatara[2] (all things are nothing but phenomena in mind); hence they are called imperceptible and unknowable. What are the perceptible and knowable phenomena?

"Not knowing that these imperceptible and unknowable phenomena are of their own minds, men from their habitual delusions invest them with an existence outside of mind, as perceptible mental phenomena, as things visible, audible, etc. These phenomena are called perceptible and knowable.

"Though there are thus two kinds, perceptible and imperceptible phenomena, they occur upon the same things, and are inseparably bound together even in the smallest particle. The difference in appearance is caused only be differences, both in mental phenomena and in the depth of conviction. Those who know only the perceptible things, without knowing the imperceptible, attached the unenlightened by Buddha...

"In contradistinction to the fallacious phenomena, there is the true Essence of Mind. Underlying the phenomena

---

Ananda, in which Sakyamuni instructs his distinguished disciple in ideas concerning the subjective and objective phenomena of mind.

1 Bodhisattvas — greatly enlightened disciples.

2 *Vidya Matra Siddhi*, a work by Vasubandhu, a native of Radjagriha, and disciple of Nagarjuna, founder of the Mahayana school. (Compare Eitel's *Handbook of Chinese Buddhism*.)

of mind, there is an unchanging principle which we call essence of mind ... The essence of mind is the entity with our ideas and with our phenomena, and is always the same. It pervades all things, and is pure and unchanging ... The essence and the phenomena of mind are inseparable; and as the former is all-pervading and ever-existing, so the phenomena occur everywhere and continually, wherever suitable conditions accompany it. Thus the perceptible and imperceptible phenomena manifestations of the essence of mind that, according to the number and nature of conditions, develop without restraint. All things in the universe, therefore, are mind itself.

"*By this we do not mean that all things combine into a unity called mind, nor that all things are emanations from it, but that, without changing their places or appearance, they are mind itself everywhere. Buddha saw this truth and said that the whole universe was his own. Hence it is clear that where the essence of mind is found, and the necessary conditions accompany it, the phenomena of mind never fail to appear...*

"*Though there is a distinction between the essence and phenomena of mind, yet they are nothing but one and the same substance, that is mind. So we say that there exists nothing but the mind. Though both the world of the pure and impure, and the generation of all things, are very wide and deep, yet they owe their existence to our minds.*"

Perhaps we might appropriately indicate that however interesting, or even fascinating, may be the distinction between "mind" and "essence of mind", in relation to phenomena, so far as we are aware, the distinction may be implied but is never precisely stated, in the text of *The Diamond Sutra*.

Nevertheless, we may readily appreciate the subtle intellectual movement, which endeavours to distinguish clearly between the phenomena of mind, and an unchanging principle underlying it, capable of being defined as Essence of Mind. Yet we have an idea that our Japanese friends intuitively find in their beautiful concept, infinitely more of a spiritual nature, than they attempt to express by the more metaphysical term. Doubtless they have frequently applied it to the more incisive logic of Sakyamuni Buddha, and found simultaneously, that what is ordinarily referred to as "essence mind" is not in reality "essence of mind," it is merely termed "essence of mind."[1]

The term "Buddha," as defined in *The Diamond Sutra*, seems to merit a brief consideration. For our present purpose it seems unnecessary to enter into questions regarding the historical Buddha, or to the authenticity of Sutras attached to his genius. Therefore, without indicating any particular reservation, we meantime accept the traditional statements that the Buddha of *The Diamond Sutra* was the son of Suddhodana, the husband of Yasodhara, and the father of Rahula. There is however, incorporated within the text, a lofty spiritual concept embodied in the familiar term Buddha, which seems to place it in a category where fresh interest is imparted to the question of its interpretation.

Concluding the twenty-sixth chapter of *The Diamond Sutra*, wherein the spiritual body[2] is entirely differentiated from external phenomena, Sakyamuni, replying to a query regarding the possibility of perceiving Buddha by means of his bodily distinctions, delivered the following remarkable Gatha[3] :—

---

 1 Compare the process of reasoning which permeates the entire *Diamond Sutra*. We hope no injustice is done to our Japanese friends, by applying, to their beautiful concept "essence of mind," this familiar logical method of Sakyamuni Buddha.

 2 Fah-Shen — the Law, or spiritual body. Compare Shen-Shen, the term usually employed in the Chinese rendering of the New Testament scriptures to denote the spiritual body.

 3 Gatha — usually a scripture of verse comprising four lines.

INTRODUCTION

I am not meant to be perceived by any visible form,
Nor sought after by means of any audible sound;
Whosoever walks in the way of iniquity,
Cannot perceive the blessedness of the Lord Buddha.[1]

In the twenty-ninth chapter of The Diamond Sutra, wherein is expounded "the majesty of the absolute," Sakyamuni declares that a disciple who affirms that "Buddha" comes or goes, obviously has not understood the meaning of his instruction. This is because, as we learn from our text, the idea "Buddha" implies neither coming from anywhere, nor going to anywhere. This purely spiritual Buddha concept seems to have seized the imagination and inspired the writer of the Yuen-Chioh Sutra,[2] to whom are subscribed the following lines:—

"*Like drifting clouds, like the waning moon, like ships that sail the ocean, like shores washed away — these are symbols of endless change. But the blessed Buddha, in his essential, absolute nature, is changeless and everlasting.*"

Again, in the seventeenth chapter of The Diamond Sutra, it is declared that, in the word "Buddha," every Law is intelligibly comprehended.[3] To Western minds, it

---

[1] Compare the following lines from *The Song Celestial*:
"*I am not known,*
To evil doers, . . . nor to those
Whose mind is cheated by the show of things."

[2] In Buddhist phraseology, Yuen-Chioh means the study of primary spiritual causes, by means of contemplation.

[3] Compare Beal's rendering in the Kin-Kong-King, "Tathagata is the explanation as it were of all systems of Law." See also *The Book of the Manifesting of the One and Manifold* in *The Song Celestial*, the verse commencing :—
"*Thou, of all souls the Soul!*
The comprehending whole!"

In conversation with Chinese monks regarding the meaning of this impressive passage, we found that they invariably

might become necessary to resist a natural inclination to ascribe to those elements of thought, an influence which had its inception in a nation other than the Indian.[1] But, lest we should appear to detract from the native glory of Sakyamuni Buddha, perhaps it might prove opportune to remark that there is sufficient evidence in the ancient *Vedic* hymns, *Upanishads*, etc., to indicate clearly the probable starting-points in the evolution of his thought. It seems to be to the everlasting humour of some early Indian philosophers, that they endeavoured carefully to combine in an abstract spiritual unity, all the elements usually combined under the term "Divinity."[2]

This may explain why the devout Buddhist, possessing a natural mental tendency induced by persistent Hindu influence, may regard "Buddha"[3] in a purely spiritual sense, as the One[4] in whom all Laws are

---

approved of a suggested rendering, that "Buddha is the One in whom all Laws become intelligible."

1 Compare the observations made by Sir Edwin Arnold in his preface to *The Song Celestial*, regarding the date when that famous Brahmanic poem was composed; and the gentle indication that in its teaching may be found "echoes of the lessons of Galilee, and of the Syrian incarnation."

2 An instructive exposition of this subject by J. Muir, Esq., entitled *The Progress of the Vedic Religion towards Abstract Conceptions of the Deity*, may be consulted in the *Journal of the Royal Asiatic Society*, 1864-65.

3 In colloquial Chinese there is a noteworthy saying, that "Buddha is simply a condition of mind." This "condition of mind" is beautifully expressed by a "classic" couplet, which, rendered into English, means "as pure as the image of a moon in a river," and "as lovely as the bloom of a flower in a mirror." (Shui-Li-Chï-Yueh, Ching-Li-Chï-Wha.)

4 Compare the beautifully expressed sentiment of Akhenaton, Pharaoh of Egypt, concerning "the One in whom all Laws are intelligibly comprehended" and "There is no poverty for him who hath Thee in his heart." (See *Life and Times of Akhenaton*).

comprehended and become perfectly intelligible.

Incidental reference is made by Buddha in *The Diamond Sutra* to the doctrines of Karma and Rebirth. It seems an old truth to which expression is also given in the *New Testament* Epistle to the Galatians; "Whatsoever a man soweth, that shall he also reap. For he that soweth to his flesh shall of the flesh reap corruption; but he that soweth to the Spirit shall of the Spirit reap life everlasting."[1]

To the Buddhist mind, Karma is indissolubly associated with "the Law which moves to Righteousness." Thus it is accustomed to view the traditional Christian idea of "justification by Faith" as a devoutly-conceived theory, rather than a reasonably constructed truth.

Occasionally we have heard a gentle affirmation, that the Western mind seems unwittingly inclined to confound the doctrine of Karma with a concept which is almost suggestive of fatalism. If Karma contains even a germ of thought which corresponds to "blind fatalism," the idea is perhaps quite fallaciously expressed in the following sentences culled from a valued letter written by an aged Chinese monk: "Karma is a universal Law which binds us to the rhythmic cycle of evolving life. It operates so quietly and imperceptibly that we scarcely are conscious of its presence. The ultimate truth of Karma greatly attracts our minds, which approve naturally of its

---

[1] Rhys Davids, when he expounded the doctrine of Karma in *Buddhism*, clearly indicated the Buddhist position, "that whatever a man reaps, that he must also have sown." Chinese Buddhists appear to be assured, "that if a man reaps sorrow, disappointment, pain, he himself and no other must at some time have sown folly, error, sin; and if not in this life, then in some former birth. Where then, in the latter case, is the identity between him who sows and him who reaps? *In that which alone remains* when a man dies, and the constituent parts of the sentient being are dissolved; in the result, namely, of his action, speech, and thought, in his good and evil *Karma* (literally his 'doing') which *does not* die.

consummate justice and perfect righteousness."

The ideas of "consummate justice" and "perfect righteousness" seem to be faithfully portrayed in the following quotation, gleaned from *The Light of Asia*:—

> *"What have been bringeth, what shall be, and is,*
> *Worse — better — last for first and first for last:*
> *The Angels in the Heavens of Gladness reap*
> *Fruits of a holy past."*

It would therefore appear that Karma may be regarded generally, as comprising the constituent moral elements derived consecutively from the thoughts, words, and actions of an interminable cycle of life. Perhaps it is in this connection that Chinese Buddhists frequently assume Karma to resemble "a moral fibre, indissolubly entwined in sentient life." It may be believed to recede far into the past, and to extend indefinitely into the future.

Although realising the significance of Karma,[1] the devout Buddhist mind is not usually disturbed by fearful forebodings. Ostensibly, it has evolved to a condition of holiness, wherein "the dross of sin" is entirely consumed in the "white flames" of Sakyamuni's "transcendent wisdom" and "boundless love."

Within the realm of Buddhist philosophy, the doctrine of rebirth is conspicuous by reason of its peculiarly attractive charms. On first acquaintance, the European mind may be startled to discover that a satisfactory explanation of the interminable evolution of life is, by learned Buddhists, sought for in the theory of rebirth.

In the text of *The Diamond Sutra*, it may be observed

---

[1] In the concept Karma, Sakyamuni Buddha suggested the revealing of a *moral cause* which explained the otherwise insoluble riddle of the evident inequalities, and consequent sufferings, of life.

that Sakyamuni Buddha, in his discourse with Subhuti, referred to personal reminiscences, one of which belonged incidentally to a distant period of five hundred incarnations.

According to the text of *The Light of Asia*, the spiritual consciousness of Sakyamuni Buddha extended to a period even more remote, as may be judged by these lines:—

> "I now remember, myriad rains ago,
> What time I roamed Himăla's hanging woods."

In briefly considering the doctrine of rebirth, perhaps it might readily be conceded to our Buddhist friends, exemplified in the Founder of the faith, a wonderful potency of intellect, and a marvellous degree of spiritual intuition. Quite agreeable, also, may be the suggestion, that the potency of intellect might become intensified, and probably "rendered subjective" by "ascetic exercises," abstract contemplation, and "determined effort."

Spence Hardy in *Eastern Monarchism* indicates that the Buddhist mind conceives of "spiritual powers" arising from the "potency of intellect" and "spiritual intuition," which in other systems of religion are usually regarded as partaking of the nature of "Divinity." If it be admitted that those potential "powers" are probably susceptible to affiliation with the Divine Spirit, that the way of approach to an understanding of the Buddhist theory of intuition becomes, perhaps, tolerably clear. Concrete knowledge acquired by intuition appears to assure our Buddhist friends of the *fact* of rebirth. But they invariably refrain from vain attempts to *prove* the "fact," by an authorised and consequently stereotyped reasoning process.

The unknown Hindu author of The Bhagavad-Gita revealed the idea of reincarnation in simple phraseology, and suggested that instructive theory regarding the advent of great Teachers and Saviours in every age. To Krishna are ascribed the following sayings:

> *"Manifold have been the renewals of*
> *my Birth... When Righteousness*
> *Declines, O Bharata, when Wickedness*
> *Is strong, I rise, from age to age, and take*
> *Visible shape, and move as man with men,*
> *Succouring the good, thrusting back the evil,*
> *And setting Virtue on her seat again."*

Rhys Davids justly observed that "it is a constant source of joy and gratitude to the pious Buddhist that the Buddha, not only at that time but in many former births, when emancipation from all the cares and trouble of life was already within his reach, should again and again, in mere love for man, have condescended to enter the world, and live amongst the sorrows inseparable from finite existence."[1] Perhaps, in a more general sense, the idea of reincarnation appealed strongly to the imagination of Wordsworth, when he was inspired to write these familiar, yet exquisite, lines:—

> *"Our birth is but a sleep and a forgetting;*
> *The soul that rises within us, our life's star,*
> *Hath had elsewhere its setting*
> *And cometh from afar."*

Regarding the doctrines of Individuality and non-Individuality, which characterise the text of *The Diamond Sutra*, wherein are found to occur frequently Chinese equivalents for the ordinary concepts of an entity, a being, a living being and a personality, the following passage from The *Bhagavad-Gita*, suggestive almost

---

1 Compare *Buddhism*. EITEL

INTRODUCTION   xxxi

of complete harmony with the Buddhist doctrine, may serve to make even a cursory consideration of the subject perhaps more illuminating. The passage, rendered by Sir Edwin Arnold, is as follows:

> "There is a 'true' Knowledge, Learn thou in this:
> To see one changeless Life in all the Lives,
> And in the Separate, One Inseparable,
> There is imperfect Knowledge; that which sees
> The separate existence apart,
> And, being separated, holds them real."

As Nirvana is only referred to casually in *The Diamond Sutra*, that familiar Buddhist term hardly calls for any present detailed explanation. Within a brief compass, probably no better explanation may be forthcoming than what is already given in this concise exposition from *The Light of Asia*:—

> "If any teach Nirvana is to cease,
> Say unto such they lie.
> If any teach Nirvana is to live,
> Say unto such they err; not knowing this,
> Nor what light shines beyond their broken lamps,
> Nor lifeless, timeless bliss."

In concluding, it might be opportune to observe that the *Werthurtheile*,[1] known amongst theologians as characterising the teachings of Albrecht Ritschl, sounds, upon intimate acquaintance, as a faint echo of

---

1 "The much-canvassed Ritschlian doctrine of the *Worth* — or "value-judgements, in which the peculiarity of religious knowledge is supposed to lie." For the introduction of the term into theology we are indebted to Herrmann, *Die Religion*, etc, and Kaftan, *Das Wesen*. See Orr's, *The Ritschlian Theology and The Evangelical Faith*.

the logic of Sakyamuni Buddha. Ritschl might apply his *Werthurtheile* to the presumed interpretation of a "miracle," etc; whereas Buddha suggested by his "method," that what is ordinarily referred to as a "miracle," is not in *reality* a "miracle," therefore it is merely *defined* as a "miracle."

So, also, with the various dogmas that distinguish every religious creed. It is regarded by many Chinese as evidence of Divinity, that in the mind of Sakyamuni Buddha there was conceived this incisive logical method; and amongst the learned monks, profound knowledge is rendered, and much wonder expressed, because the Lord Buddha[1] did not hesitate to apply his principles to every doctrine synonymous with his own accredited "Law."

---

1 In this English version of *The Diamond Sutra*, it may be observed that the Chinese term Fuh, in deference to our Chinese friends, is invariably rendered "Lord Buddha" — a designation consistent with their concepts of devotion and piety.

THE DIAMOND SUTRA

Thus have I heard[1] concerning our Lord Buddha —
Upon a memorable occasion, the Lord Buddha[2] sojourned in the kingdom of Shravasti,[3] lodging in the grove of Jeta,[4] a park within the imperial domain,

---

1 It is generally supposed that the familiar introductory phrase, "Thus have I heard," was adopted by writers or editors of Buddhist Sutras, in order that their scriptures might assume the same high degree of authority as the Brahmanas and the Mantras, "as forming the 'S'ruti' of sacred revelation of the followers of the Vedas." (Compare Max Möller's *History of Sanscrit Literature* and the valuable note in Samuel Beal's *Kin-Kong-King*.)

2 "The term (Buddha) means 'every intelligent being who has thrown off the bondage of sense perception and self, knows the utter unreality of phenomena, and is ready to enter Nirvana.'" – *Handbook of Chinese Buddhism*. EITEL

3 Shravasti is variously described as the city (or kingdom) of philosophy, of good doctrine, of abundant virtue, and as the abode of immortals. It was situated on the north bank of the Ganges, about 200 miles above Benares. Much interesting information regarding the sacred city of Shravasti is fortunately preserved in the instructive records of the distinguished Chinese pilgrims, *Fa-Hien* and *Hiuen-Tsang*.

4 "Prasenajit, the king of Shravasti, was very favourable to the Buddhist religion. It was his minister who bought the

which Jeta, the heir apparent, bestowed upon Sutana,[1] a benevolent Minister of State, renowned for his charities and benefactions.

With the Lord Buddha, there were assembled together twelve hundred and fifty mendicant disciples,[2] all of whom had attained to eminent degrees of spiritual wisdom.

As it approached the hour of the morning meal, Lord Buddha, Honoured of the Worlds,[3] attired himself in a mendicant's robe,[4] and

---

garden of Jeta from the Prince of that name, and erected in it a residence for Buddha (see Julien's *Memoires sur-les Contrées Occidentalees*). Many of the Sutras attributed to Buddha are said to have been delivered here. Hiuen-Tsang observed the remains of the monastery formerly standing on the site of the garden of Jeta, two miles below the city." — *Chinese Buddhism.* EDKINS

1 "A person of extraordinary piety and goodness. One of the former Djatakas of Sakyamuni when he was a prince, and forfeited the throne by liberality in alms-giving." — *Handbook of Chinese Buddhism.* EITEL

2 The Chinese text is *ta-pi-ku* — greater disciples. Our Chinese editor of *The Diamond Sutra* suggests that there are different grades of discipleship. The "lesser disciples" are those who have abandoned every form of vice, and are striving after virtue. The "greater disciples" are those to whom virtue has become spontaneous, and who have ceased to strive after its attainment.

3 A title conferred by Chinese Buddhists, believing him to be a Teacher, indeed Saviour whose merit is acclaimed in worlds beyond our own.

4 Having taken vows of poverty, a robe is one of the following eight articles which Buddhist monks are permitted to possess: three garments of different descriptions, a girdle for the loins, an alms bowl, a razor, a needle, and a water-strainer.

bearing an alms-bowl in his hands, walked towards the great city of Shravasti, which he entered to beg for food.¹ Within the city he proceeded from door to door,² and received such donations as the good people severally bestowed.³ Concluding this religious exercise, the Lord Buddha returned to the grove of Jeta, and partook of the frugal meal ⁴ received as alms. Thereafter he divested himself of his

---

1 Buddha has said, "the wise priest never asks for anything; he disdains to beg; it is a proper thing for which he carries the alms-bowl; and this is his only mode of solicitation. But, when he is sick, he is permitted to ask for any medicine that he may require, without being guilty of any transgression." — *Eastern Monachism.* SPENCE HARDY

2 Concerning the manner of begging an alms: "As a bee, injuring not the flower. or its colour, or its scent, flies away, taking the nectar, so let a sage go through the village." — *Questions of King Milinda.* RHYS DAVIDS

3 "By many of the Buddhists it is considered to be an act of great merit to make a vow never to partake of food without giving a portion to the priests." — *Eastern Monachism.* SPENCE HARDY

4 The fifth of the twelve sacred observances of the Chinese is called in Sanscrit 'Khaloupas Waddhaktinka', and is said to enjoin that the food obtained by the mendicant is to be divided into three portions: one to be given to any person he sees to be suffering from hunger, and a second to be carried to some quiet place in the forest, and placed on a stone for the birds and beasts. If he does not meet with anyone who is in want, he is not to eat the whole of the food he has received, but two-thirds only. By this means his body will be lighter and more active. He will be able readily to enter upon the practice of all good works. When any one eats too greedily . . . nothing is more harmful to the development of reason." (Quotation from Remusat's *Relation des Royaumes Buddhiques*, in Spence Hardy's *Eastern Monachism*).

mendicant's robe, laid aside the venerated alms-bowl,[1] bathed his sacred feet, and accepted the honoured seat reserved for him by his disciples.

Upon that occasion, the venerable Subhuti [2] occupied a place in the midst of the assembly. Rising from his seat, with cloak arranged in such manner that his right shoulder was disclosed, Subhuti knelt upon his right knee, then pressing together the palms of his hands, he respectfully raised them towards Lord Buddha, saying: "Thou art of transcendent wisdom, Honoured of the Worlds! With wonderful solicitude, Thou dost preserve in the faith, and instruct in the Law, this illustrious assembly of enlightened disciples.[3] Honoured of the Worlds! If a good

---

1 "The alms-bowl which Sakyamuni used is considered a sacred relic, to be used by each of the hundred Buddhas of the present kalpa. It was first preserved in Vais'ali, whence its emigrations began to Gandhara, to Persia, to China, to Ceylon, to Madhyades'a, up into the heaven Tuchita, and down to the bottom of the ocean, where it is to await (in the palace of Sagara) the advent of Meitraya Buddha." — *Handbook of Chinese Buddhism*. EITEL

2 A famous dialectician noted for the subtlety of his intellect. He was a native of Shravasti, a contemporary of Sakyamuni, and figures as the principal interlocutor in the *Prajna-Paramita*." — *Handbook of Chinese Buddhism* EITEL

3 *Pu-Sa* or Bodhisattva, literally he whose essence (Sattva) has become intelligence (Bodhi). A being that has only once

disciple, whether man or woman,[1] seeks to obtain supreme spiritual wisdom,[2] what immutable Law shall sustain the mind of that disciple, and bring into subjection every inordinate desire?"[3]

The Lord Buddha replied to Subhuti, saying: "Truly a most excellent theme! As you affirmed, I preserve in the faith, and instruct in the Law, this illustrious assembly of enlightened disciples. Attend diligently

---

more to pass through human existence before it attains to Buddhaship. The third class of Buddhistic saints comprehending all who are candidates for Buddhaship, as well as those Buddhas who are not yet perfected by entrance to Nirvana. They are also styled Mahasattvas (*Mo-Ho-Sa*). The state of a Bodhisattva is considered one of the three means of conveyance to Nirvana"
— *Handbook of Chinese Buddhism* EITEL

1 "Women began to ask and receive permission to take the vows. They were called in India 'Bikshuni' . . . 'ni' is the Sanscrit feminine termination of Bikshu. These female mendicants were subject to the same code of regulations as the males." *Chinese Buddhism* EDKINS

2 "h*o-ru-to-lo-san-mao-san-pu-ti* (Anuttara Samyak Sambodhi), literally unexcelled, perfect intelligence. Another more painstaking but arbitrary explanation is untarnished and unparalleled (Nuttara) correct view (Sam) and complete wisdom (Myak), with complete possession of the highest sentiments (Sambodhi). This term, one of the sacred phrases of most frequent occurrence, signifies the characteristics which every Buddha possesses." — *Handbook of Chinese Buddhism* EITEL,

Also, "The unsurpassed, just and enlightened heart."
— *Kin-Kong-King* BEAL

3 "When a man's heart is disposed in accordance with his roaming senses, it snatches away his spiritual knowledge as the wind does a ship on the waves." — *Bhagavad-Gita*
COCKBURN THOMSON

unto me, and I shall enunciate a Law whereby the mind of a good disciple, whether man or woman, seeking to obtain supreme spiritual wisdom,[1] and enabled to bring into subjection every inordinate desire." Subhuti was gratified, and signified glad consent. Thereupon, the Lord Buddha, with majesty of person,[2] and perfect articulation, proceeded to deliver the text of this Scripture,[3] saying:—

❋ ❋ ❋ ❋ ❋

"By this wisdom shall enlightened disciples be enabled to bring into subjection every inordinate desire! Every species of life, whether hatched in the egg, formed in the womb, evolved from spawn, produced by metamorphosis, with or without form or intelligence, possessing or devoid of natural instinct — from these changeful[4] conditions

---

1 Chinese commentators are careful to explain that the title of this Sutra, *Po-Ro-Po-Lo-Mi* (*Prajna-Paramita*), means Wisdom, by which we are enabled to reach the other shore (Nirvana).

2 Compare the Chinese text of the famous Buddhist tract entitled *Awakening of Faith* written by *Ma-Ming* (Asvaghocha), "who flourished A.D. 50, under the Indo-Scythic king, Gondophares."

3 "This work contains the germ of the larger compilation Prajna-Paramita in one hundred and twenty volumes. The abstractions of Buddhist philosophy, which were afterwards ramified to such a formidable extent as these numbers indicate, are here found in their primary form, probably as they were taught by Sakyamuni himself." *Chinese Buddhism* EDKINS

4 Discoursing upon illusory ideas concerning the world of

THE DIAMOND SUTRA 7

of being, I command you to seek deliverance[1] in the transcendental concept of Nirvana.[2] Thus, you shall be delivered from an immeasurable, innumerable, and illimitable world of sentient life; but, in reality, there is no world of sentient life from which to seek deliverance. And why? Because, in the

---

sentient life, the Lord Buddha stated that these were already eliminated from the minds of his enlightened disciples. The reference in the text is to disciples in process of instruction, and these the Lord Buddha commanded to relegate to oblivion the deceptive idea of the reality of sentient life, to dissolve within their minds its nauseous dregs, to put away its horrid stain, and cause it to vanish like snow in a glowing furnace. – *Chinese Annotation*.

1 By adopting the terms *Mieh-Tu*, Chinese Buddhists appear well prepared to refute a prevalent notion that their concept of deliverance is equivalent to annihilation. *Mieh* usually means annihilation, but *Tu*, to cross over in safety, is the antithesis of annihilation. After due consideration of the significance of the terminology, it may be generally conceded that English renderings of *Mieh-Tu* as Deliverance or Salvation, are not without some degree of justification.

2 "Dewdrop slips into shining sea." *Light of Asia* ARNOLD.

"The dewdrop re-becomes the shining sea." — *Chioh-Hsien* (a Chinese monk). Also, "The popular exoteric systems agree in defining Nirvana negatively as a state of absolute exemption from the circle of transmigration; as a state of freedom from all forms of materiality, from all passion and exertion, mentally and emotionally, a state of indifference therefore alike to joy and pain. Positively they define Nirvana as the highest stage of spiritual liberty and bliss, as absolute immortality through absorption of the soul into itself. Individuality is preserved, and Buddhas who have entered Nirvana occasionally reappear again to intervene on behalf of the faithful." *Handbook of Chinese Buddhism* EITEL

minds[1] of enlightened disciples there have ceased to exist such arbitrary concepts of phenomena as an entity, a being, a living being, or a personality.[2]

"Moreover, Subhuti, an enlightened disciple ought to act spontaneously in the

---

1 The able commentator *Ti-Ching* observes that many people like Ananda, a favourite disciple of Buddha, are in error when they suppose their minds to be located within their material bodies. This interesting aspect of Buddhist psychology is made tolerably clear in the familiar narrative known generally as "*The Enlightenment of Ananda.*" Therein the Lord Buddha endeavours to prove that as objects within ourselves are invisible, the illuminating mind cannot be asserted to inhabit exclusively our material bodies. He indicates also that it cannot be affirmed to occupy any appointed sphere outside ourselves, it being usually understood that we observe only those objects by which we are environed. The Lord Buddha also controverts the theory, enunciated by Ananda, that the mind is secreted elsewhere within the organs of sense; which assumption is based on a notion that the seeing eye and the differentiated mind are mysteriously correlated.

2 This belief in self is regarded so distinctly as a heresy that two well-known words in Buddhist terminology have been coined in order to stigmatise it. The first of these is *Sakkayaditthi*, The heresy of individuality," the name given to this belief as one of the three primary delusions (the others being doubt, and belief in the efficacy of rites or ceremonies) which must be abandoned at the very first stage of the Buddhist path of holiness. The other is *Attavada*, "the doctrine of soul or self," which is the name given to it as part of the chain of causes which lead to the origin of evil. It is there classed along with sensuality, heresy (as to eternity and annihilation), and belief in the efficacy of rites and ceremonies — as one of the four *Upadanas*, which are the immediate cause of birth, decay, death, sorrow, lamentation, pain, grief and despair." —*Buddhism* RHYS DAVIDS

exercise of charity,[1] uninfluenced by sensitive phenomena[2] such as sound, odour, taste, touch or Law.[3] Subhuti, it is imperative that an enlightened disciple, in the exercise of charity, should act independently of phenomena. And why? Because, acting without regard to illusive forms of phenomena, he will realise in the exercise of charity, a merit inestimable and immeasurable.

---

1 "The first of six Paramita — charity, morality, endurance, energy, contemplation and wisdom — cardinal virtues, or means of progressing towards Nirvana. The virtue of religious charity, implying all kinds of self-denying acts, almsgiving, sacrifice, etc." — *Handbook of Chinese Buddhism.* EITEL

2 "The kind of craving excitement, which follows on sensation, causing the delusion of self and the lust of life — creating either delight in the objects that present themselves, or an eager desire to supply a felt want. This eager yearning or 'thirst' growing into sensuality, desire of future life, or love of the present world, is the cause of all suffering. Sorrow and suffering will be overcome, extinguished, if this 'thirst' be quenched, this lust of life destroyed. 'He who overcomes this contemptible thirst, sufferings fall off from him like water drops from a lotus leaf.'" — *Buddhism* RHYS DAVIDS

3 *Fah*, the Chinese equivalent of Dharma — Law, appraise to be a generic term for all religious doctrines incidental to Buddhism. The Buddhas are invariably referred to as *Fah-Wang* — Princes of the Law, The Sutras a frequently alluded to as *Fah-Pao* — Jewels of the Law. The Monks are usually designated *Fah-Men* — Disciples of the Law. The interminable process of transmigration is depicted by *Fah-Luen* — Wheel of the Law. The dissemination of Buddhistic tenets is typified by *Chuan-Fah-Luon* — Revolving Wheel of the Law. Religious designations consonant with the idea of Law, are held high in the esteem amongst the Buddhist ecclesiastical orders. Of such are *Fah-Ai* — Lover of the Law; *Fah-Ming* — Brightness of the Law.

"Subhuti, what think you? Is it possible to estimate the distance comprising the illimitable universe of space?"[1] Subhuti replied: "Honoured of the Worlds! It is impossible to estimate the distance comprising the illimitable universe of space." The Lord Buddha thereupon discoursed, saying: "It is equally impossible to estimate the merit[2] of an enlightened disciple, who exercises the discharge of charity, unperturbed by the seductive influences of phenomena. Subhuti, the mind of an enlightened disciple ought thus to

---

1 "Subhuti, can the western, or southern, or eastern, or northern regions of space be measured? Or the four midway regions of space (ie, N.E., S.E., S.W., N.W.), or the upper and lower regions: can either of these be accurately measured or defined?" — *Kin-Kong-King*. BEAL.

2 Of all the modes of acquiring merit, that of almsgiving is the principal; it is the chief of the virtues that are requisite for the attainment of Buddhaship; it is the first of the four great virtues, *viz*: almsgiving, affability, promoting the prosperity of others, and loving others as ourselves. It is superior to the observances of the precepts — the path that all the Buddhas have trod — a lineage to which they have all belonged...The giving of alms softens the mind, and brings it into subjection, by which the ascetic is prepared for the exercise of the rites he is afterwards to practise... The faithful are required to give in alms that which they have honestly earned by their own personal exertions... There must be a willing mind respecting that which they offer, from the time that the intention of making the offering is formed to the time when it is presented, as well as after it has been made. . . When the gift, the giver and the receiver are all pure, the reward is proportionately great." — *Eastern Monachism*. SPENCE HARDY.

be indoctrinated." [1]

The Lord Buddha interrogated Subhuti, saying: "What think you? Is it possible that by means of his physical body,[2] the Lord Buddha may be clearly perceived?" Subhuti replied, saying: "No! Honoured of the Worlds! It is impossible that by means of his physical body, the Lord Buddha may be clearly perceived. And why? Because, what the Lord Buddha referred to as physical body, is in reality not merely a physical body." Thereupon the Lord Buddha addressed Subhuti, saying:

---

1   *"Let his livelihood be kindliness,*
    His conduct righteousness,
    Then in the fullness of gladness
    He will make an end of grief." — Buddhism. RHYS DAVIDS

2   "Primitive Buddhism distinguished a material, visible, and perishable body (*Seh-Shen* — lit., the Body of Form) and an immaterial, invisible, immortal body (*Fah-Shen* — Lit., the Body of Law) as the constituents of every personality. This dichotomism, taught, as it seems by Sakyamuni himself, was ever afterwards retained as regards the nature of ordinary mortals. But in later ages, when the combined influence of Sivaism, which ascribed to Siva a threefold body (called *Dharmakaya* — essence, *Sambhogakaya* — reflex intelligence, and *Nirmanakaya* — practical issue of his intelligence), and that of Brahmanism with its Trimurti, gave rise to the Buddhist dogma of a Triratna (*San-Pao* — the precious Buddha, the precious Law, and the previous Priesthood), trichotomism was taught with regard to the nature of all Buddhas. Again they ascribed to every Buddha a triple form of existence, viewing him: (1) as having entered Nirvana; (2) as existing in reflex in the world of form; (3) as existing or having existed on earth." — *Handbook of Chinese Buddhism*. EITEL.

"Every form or quality of phenomena is transient and illusive. When the mind realises that the phenomena of life are not real phenomena, the Lord Buddha may then be entirely perceived."[1]

Subhuti enquired of the Lord Buddha, saying: "Honoured of the Worlds! In future ages, when this scripture is proclaimed, amongst those beings destined to hear, shall any conceive within their minds a sincere, un-mingled faith?"[2]

The Lord Buddha replied to Subhuti, saying: "Have no such apprehensive thought! Even at the remote period of five centuries subsequent to the Nirvana of the Lord Buddha[3] there will be many disciples observing the monastic vows,[4] and assiduously devoted to

---

1 The spiritual Buddha must be realised within the mind, otherwise there can be no true perception of the Lord Buddha. — *Chinese Annotation*.

2 Compare the question addressed by Jesus Christ to his disciples, "When the Son of Man cometh, shall He find faith on earth?"

3   "In the fullness of the times — it fell
    The Buddha died, the great Tathagata,
    Even as a man 'mongst men, fulfilling all:
    And how a thousand thousand lakhs since then
    Have trod the path whither he went
    Unto Nirvana, where the Silence lives." — *The Light of Asia*. ARNOLD.

4 When a novice seeks admission to a monastic order, an

good works.[1] These, hearing this scripture proclaimed, will believe in its immutability, and similarly conceive within their minds a pure, unmingled faith. Besides, it is important to realise that faith[2] thus conceived, is not exclusively in virtue of the insular thought of any particular Buddha, but because of its affiliation with the concrete[3] thoughts of myriad Buddhas, throughout infinite ages. Therefore, amongst the beings destined to hear this Scripture proclaimed, many, by momentary reflection, will intuitively[4]

---

ordination service is conducted by a chapter of monks, at which the following vows are administered. "I take the vow not to destroy life. I take the vow not to steal. I take the vow to abstain from impurity. I take the vow not to lie. I take the vow to abstain from intoxicating drinks, which hinder progress and virtue. I take the vow not to eat at forbidden times. I take the vow to abstain from dancing, singing, music and stage plays. I take the vow not to use garlands, scents, unguents, or ornaments. I take the vow not to use a high or broad bed. I take the vow not to receive gold or silver." (Compare *Buddhism*. RHYS DAVIDS).

1 "The primary motive for doing good, and worshipping Buddha, according to these scriptures (the Buddha scriptures of Nepal), is the hope of attaining absorption into the nature of the god, and being freed from transgressions — *China*. DAVIS

2   "*And is thy faith so much to give,*
    Is it a thing so hard to see,
    That the Spirit of God, whate'er it be,
    The Law that abides and changes not, ages long,
    The Eternal and Nature-Born — these things be strong?"

— *The Bacche*. EURIPIDES (Trans. Gilbert Murray)

3 The elements of faith, like the flowers, appear to have their roots in eternity." — *Chang-Ming* (a Chinese monk).

4 "Were it possible for a Yogi and a Rahat from India, a Greek

conceive a pure and holy faith.

"Subhuti, the Lord Buddha by his prescience,[1] is perfectly cognisant of all such potential disciples, and for those also is reserved an immeasurable merit. And why? Because, the minds of these disciples will not revert to such arbitrary concepts of phenomena as an entity, a being, a living being, a personality, qualities of ideas coincident with the Law, or existing apart from the idea of Law. And why? Because, assuming the permanency and reality of phenomena, the minds of these disciples would be involved in such distinctive ideas as an entity, a being,

---

philosopher from one of the schools holding the power of intuition, an ascetic from the wilds of Syria or the mountains of Egypt, a heretic from the school at Alexandria, a monk from one of the monasteries of Europe, a schoolman of the Middle Ages, and a modern German metaphysician of the school of Schelling to meet together, and were it possible for them to forget their sectarian subtleties and nice distinctions, they would find there was a vast mass of speculation about the main principles of which they were agreed. They would be of one mind relative to the four following propositions: (1) That there is an objective potency of intellect; (2) That this potency can be rendered subjective by concentrated thought, ascetic exercises, or determined effort; (3) That this potency can only be acquired by the initiated; (4) That the initiated may enlarge this potency to limitless extent. As to the efficient cause of the potency, there would be a difference of opinion: some would ascribe it to intuition alone, while others would attribute it to an alliance with high spirits or with God; but of its existence, there would be no doubt." — *Eastern Monachism*. SPENCE HARDY.

[1] *"For now I know, by what within me stirs,*
That I shall teach compassion unto man
And be a speechless world's interpreter."
— *The Light of Asia*. ARNOLD

a living being, and a personality. Affirming the permanency and reality of qualities or ideas coincident with Law, their minds would inevitably be involved in resolving these same definitions. Postulating the inviolate nature of ideas which have an existence apart from the Law, there yet remain to be explained these abstruse distinctions — an entity, a being, a living being, and a personality. Therefore, enlightened disciples ought not to affirm the permanency or reality of qualities or ideas coincident with Law, nor postulate as being of an inviolate nature, qualities or ideas having an existence apart from the concept of Law.

"Thus, we are enabled to appreciate the significance of those words which the Lord Buddha invariably repeated to his followers: 'You disciples must realise that the Law which I enunciated, was presented before your minds in the simile of a raft.[1] If the Law — having fulfilled its function in bearing you to the other shore (Nirvana)[2]

---

[1] "I have made a well-constructed raft, said Bhagavat — and passed over (to Nibbana). I have reached the further bank, having overcome the torrent (of passions). There is no (further) use for a raft; therefore, if thou like, rain, O sky!"
— *Sutta-Nipata.* FAUSBÖLL

[2] Compare the New Testament idea expressed by the apostle Paul, "wherefore the law was our schoolmaster to bring us unto Christ." Also, the that used in Christian anthology, "We shall meet on that beautiful *shore.*"

— with its coincident qualities and ideas. must inevitably be abandoned,[1] how much more inevitable must be the abandonment of qualities or ideas which have an existence apart from the Law?' "

The Lord Buddha addressed Subhuti, saying: "What think you? Has the Lord Buddha really attained to spiritual wisdom? Or has he a system of doctrine which can be specifically formulated?"

Subhuti replied, saying: "As I understand the meaning of the Lord Buddha's discourse, he has no system of doctrine which can be specifically formulated; nor can the Lord Buddha express, in explicit terms, a form of knowledge which can be described as supreme spiritual wisdom. And why? Because, what the Lord Buddha adumbrated in terms of the Law, is transcendental and inexpressible. Being a purely spiritual concept, it is neither consonant with Law, nor synonymous with anything apart from the Law. Thus[2] is exemplified the manner

---

1 "Our little systems have their day,
They have their day and cease to be;
They are but broken lights of Thee,
But thou, O Lord, art more than they." — TENNYSON

2 "So it appears that all the sages and wise men who have lived have all adopted this mode of diffusive doctrine [which

by which wise disciples and holy Buddhas, regarding intuition [1] as the Law of their minds, severally attained to different planes of spiritual wisdom." [2]

The Lord Buddha addressed Subhuti, saying: "What think you? If a benevolent person bestowed as alms the seven treasures [3] sufficient to fill the universe, would there accrue to that person considerable merit?"

Subhuti replied, saying: "A very considerable merit, Honoured of the Worlds! And why? Because, what is referred to does not partake in the nature of ordinary merit, and in this sense the Lord Buddha made mention of a considerable merit."

The Lord Buddha rejoined, saying: "If a disciple adhered with implicit faith to a single stanza [4] of this Scripture, and diligently

---

admits of no particular distinction (*wou-wei*)], and hence the differences that have occurred." — *Kin-Kong-King*. BEAL

1 The Chinese text "*i-wu-wei-fah,*" is explained by a learned expositor as *tsu-ran-choih-sing* — the intuitive faculty.

2 "Because that thing which was known or taught by the Tathagata is incomprehensible and inexpressible. It is neither a thing nor a no-thing. And why? Because the holy persons are of imperfect power." *The Vagrakkhedika*. MAX MÜLLER.

3 "Gold, silver, aquamarine, crystal, white coral, ruby and emerald."

4 "Gatha — hymns and chants, narratives containing moral expositions in metrical language. A Chinese text says, '32 characters from one Gatha,' which refers to a certain variety

explained it to others, the intrinsic merit of that disciple would be relatively greater. And why? Because, Subhuti, the holy Buddhas, and the Law[1] by which they attained to supreme spiritual wisdom, severally owe their inception to the truth[2] of this sacred Scripture. Subhuti, what is ordinarily termed the Buddha Law, is not really a Law attributive to Buddha."[3]

---

of Gatha called Aryagiti, a metre consisting of 32 instants." — *Handbook of Chinese Buddhism.* EITEL

1 "The *Dharmma* (Law) is perfect, having nothing redundant, and nothing wanting. But it requires attention, that the benefits it offers may be received. Though the teacher may attain great happiness, and enter Nirvana, it does not follow that the disciple will necessarily possess the same privileges; he may be like one who binds the crown upon the head of another. Therefore each one for himself must exercise meditation, and observe the ordinances, that he may attain wisdom." — *Eastern Monachism.* SPENCE HARDY

2 "Faith is in the world the best property for a man: *Dhamma* (the Law), well observed, conveys happiness; truth, indeed, is the sweetest of things; and the life they call the best which is lived with understanding." — *Sutta-Nipala.* FAUSBÖLL

3 "What then, Subhuti? All the Buddhas, and the perfect laws of the Buddhas, have sprung from (the principles of) this one Sutra; but, Subhuti, that which is spoken of as the Law of Buddha, is after all not such a Law (or, is a Law of no Buddha)." —*Kin-King-King.* BEAL

"Because, O Subhuti, the highest perfect knowledge of the holy and enlightened Tathagatas is produced from it; the blessed Buddhas are produced from it. And why? Because, O Subhuti, when the Tathagata preached: 'The qualities of Buddha, the qualities of Buddha indeed!' They were preached by him as no-qualities of Buddha." — *The Vagrakkhedika.* MAX MÜLLER

An erudite Chinese commentator suggests that the words

THE DIAMOND SUTRA

The Lord Buddha enquired of Subhuti, saying: "What think you? May a Scrotapatti,[1] (having entered the stream which bears onto Nirvana) thus moralise within himself, 'I have obtained the fruits[2] commensurate with the merit of a Scrotapatti?'" Subhuti replied, saying: "No! Honoured of the Worlds! And why? Because, Scrotapatti is simply a descriptive term signifying 'having entered the stream.' A disciple who avoids the seductive phenomena of form, sound, odour, taste, touch, and Law,[3] is named a Scrotapatti."

---

fei-fuh-fah are synonymous with *wu-wei-fah* — intuition, already observed in the previous section. A familiar passage from *Lao-Tsz*, "Infinite truth is inexpressible," is quoted by our commentator as serving to illustrate the difficulty of giving expression to an idea equivalent to the Law of Buddha.

1 "One who has entered (Apatti) the stream (Scrota), the latter being defined as the stream of holy conduct (which bears onto Nirvana)." — *Handbook of Chinese Buddhism.* EITEL

2 "Men walking in the path, and standing in the fruits thereof, those who have yet attained some fruits thereof but are yet learners ... Whose hope is directed to the utmost goal." — *Questions of King Milinda.*
RHYS DAVIDS

3 Perhaps in the sense that a Scrotapatti clearly perceives and understands the tentative nature of the Law, his mind being trained to regard it as "a well constructed raft,' designed to bear him safely across the stream of spiritual consciousness upon which he has entered. It also appears that the Scrotapatti discerns in the *idea* of the Law, something as unreal and ephemeral as the phenomena of form, sound, odour, taste or touch. In seeking "Nirvana's blessed abode," the Scrotapatti

The Lord Buddha again enquired of Subhuti, saying: "What think you? May a Sakridagami¹ (who is subject to only one more rebirth) thus muse within himself, 'I have obtained the fruits consonant with the merit of a Sakradagami?'" Subhuti replied, saying: "No! Honoured of the Worlds! And why? Because² Sakradagami is merely a descriptive title denoting 'only one more rebirth'; but in reality there is no such condition as 'only one more rebirth,' hence, Sakradagami is merely a descriptive title."

The Lord Buddha once again enquired of Subhuti, saying: "What think you? May an Anagami³ (having entire immunity from

---

endeavours to "rise by daily sojourn with these fantasies — to lovelier verities."

1 "The path of Sakradagami is so called because he who enters it will receive one more birth. He may enter this path in the world of men, and afterwards be born in a Dewa-Loka (a heavenly mansion —in Chinese *Tien-Kong*): or he may enter it in a Dewa-Loka, and afterwards be born in the world of men." — *Eastern Monachism*. SPENCE HARDY

2 "Because he is not an individual being (Dharma), who has obtained the state of a Sakradagami." — *The Vagrakkhedika*. MAX MÜLLER

3 "Not returning, or not being reborn in the world of desire. The third degree of Buddhistic saintship, the third class of Aryas, embracing all those who are no more liable to be reborn as men, though they are to be born once more as Devas, when they will forthwith become Arhats and enter Nirvana." — *Handbook of Chinese Buddhism*. EITEL

"Men devoid of passion, and of malice, and of dullness, men

rebirth) this reflect within himself, 'I have obtained the fruits which accord with the merit of an Anagami?'" Subhuti replied, saying: "No! Honoured of the Worlds! And why? Because, Anagami is merely a designation meaning 'immunity from rebirth'; but in reality there is no such condition as 'immunity from rebirth,' hence Anagami is merely a convenient designation."

The Lord Buddha yet again enquired of Subhuti, saying: "What think you? May an Arhat,[1] (having attained to absolute quiescence of mind) thus meditate within himself. 'I have obtained the condition of Arhat'?" Subhuti replied, saying: "No! Honoured of the Worlds!

---

in whom the great evils (lust, becoming, delusion and ignorance) are not, men who have neither craving thirst, nor grasping desires." — *Questions of King Melinda.* RHYS DAVIDS

1 "Explained by *Kuh-Ko* — the Fruit of Buddha (Buddhaphalam). The original meaning of Arhat (deserving, worthy) is overlooked by most Chinese commentators, who explained the term as if it were written *Ari-Hat* — Destroyer of the Enemy. The following two explanations are given, *Shah-Tseh* — Destroying the Enemy, and *Puh-Seng* — not to be reborn; ie, except from transmigration. There is, however, a third explanation which is based on the original meaning of Arhat, namely *Ying-Kong* — deserving worship. The Arhat is the perfected Arya (one who has mastered the four spiritual truths *Sz-Ti* and thereby entered the path to Nirvana called Arya-Marga), so that the state of Arhat can only be attained by passing through the different degrees of saintship. Arhatship implies possession of supernatural powers, and is to be succeeded either by Buddhaship or by immediate entrance into Nirvana." — *Handbook of Chinese Buddhism.* EITEL

And why? Because, there is not in reality a condition synonymous with the term Arhat. Honoured of the Worlds, if an Arhat thus meditates within himself, 'I have attained the condition of an Arhat,' there would be obvious recurrence of such arbitrary concepts as an entity, a being, a living being, and a personality. Honoured of the Worlds! When the Lord Buddha declared that in absolute quiescence[1] of mind, perfect observance of the Law,[2] and true spiritual perception, I was pre-eminent amongst the disciples, I did not cogitate thus within myself. 'I am an Arhat, freed[3] from desire!' Had I thus cogitated, 'I

---

    1 A Chinese annotator suggests it is almost self-evident that "absolute quiescence" is the condition of mind in which knowledge is acquired by intuition.

2   *"More is the treasure of the Law than gems;*
    Sweeter than comb its sweetness; its delights
    Delightful past compare." — *The Light of Asia.* ARNOLD

    3 "The man for whom there is nothing upon which he depends, who is independent, having understood the *Dhamma* (Law), for whom there is no desire for coming into existence — him I call calm . . . He has overcome desire." — *Dhammapada.* MAX MÜLLER

    And further, "This devotion should be practised with that determination by which thought becomes indifferent (to every worldly object). He who has abandoned all desires which spring from imagination, and has, by means of his heart, kept back the whole collection of the senses from every direction (in which they would go), should gradually become passive by his mind's acquiring firmness, and, by having caused his heart to remain within himself, should not place his thoughts on anything at all." — *Bhagavad-Gita.* COCKBURN THOMSON

have obtained the condition of Arhat,'[1] the Honoured of the Worlds would not have declared concerning me, 'Subhuti delights in the austerities practised by Aranyaka;[2] but, in reality, Subhuti was perfectly quiescent and oblivious to phenomena;[3] hence the allusion,

---

1 "There are some persons who obtain the Rahatship instantaneously, while others can only obtain it by a slow process; they must give alms, make offerings, study the *Bama* (Law), and exercise the necessary discipline." — *Eastern Monachism*. SPENCE HARDY

2 "Explained by 'living in retirement,' 'a hermit,' 'a recluse.' The term signifies ascetics who live in strict seclusion. There are three classes to be distinguished. The first is called *Dharma Arankaya* — 'Hermits of the Law,' their favourite tenet being the doctrine that the principles (*Dharma*) constituting human nature are originally, calm, still and passive. Their favourite tree is the Bhodi (tree of intelligence). The second class is called *Matanga Aranyaka*. Its members reside consistently in cemeteries, and are prohibited to approach a village within hearing distance of the lowing of a cow. They are probably called after the Hindu caste *Matanga*. The third class, or *Danataka Aranyaka*, is formed by hermits living on the beach or on half-tide rocks." — *Handbook of Chinese Buddhism*. EITEL

"Men whose home is the forest, man who've taken on themselves the extra vows, men full of joy, men who are wearing rough garments, men rejoicing in the solitude." — *Questions of King Melinda*. RHYS DAVIDS

3 "The *Sramana* (Buddhist monk) who sets himself to overcome the evils of existence, retires from all intercourse with the world, and either practices meditation, simply, or joins with it in the practice of Kasina (an ascetic exercise to free the mind from all agitation), by which he is enable to attain to *Nimitta* (inward illumination), represented as being a mental illumination that brings with it, in various degrees of perfection, the state of mind called *Samadhi* (absolute self-abstraction). This result of profound meditation includes undisturbed tranquillity, and equanimity the most entire, and in its superior degree

'Subhuti delights in the austerities practised by the Aranyaka.' "

The Lord Buddha addressed Subhuti, saying: "What think you? When the Lord Buddha, in a previous life, was a disciple of Dapankara [1] Buddha, was there communicated to him any prescribed Law, or system of doctrine, whereby he eventually became a Buddha?" Subhuti replied, saying: "No! Honoured of the Worlds! When the Lord Buddha was a disciple of Dipankara Buddha, neither prescribed Law nor system of doctrine was communicated to him, whereby he eventually became a Buddha." [2]

The Lord Buddha addressed Subhuti, saying: "What think you? May an enlightened

---

produces unconsciousness." — *Eastern Monachism*. SPENCE HARDY

1 "*Ran-Teng-Fu* – the Buddha who illuminates brightly: *Ting-Kwang-Fuh* – the Buddha of fixed light. The twenty-fourth predecessor of Sakyamuni, from whom he received the asurance of his being destined for Buddhaship." — *Handbook of Chinese Buddhism*. EITEL

2 "It is maintained by the Buddhists that the wisdom which was manifested by the founder of their faith was entirely αὐτοδίδακτος. The wisdom that he manifested was the out-beaming of a self-enkindled flame, not an inspiration from any external source, nor was it the result of any process of thought or reason. To whatever object he directed his intellectual vision, whether it was near or remote, whether past, present or future, he saw it in a moment, intuitively, yet in the most absolutely perfect manner." — *Eastern Monachism*. SPENCE HARDY

disciple thus ponder within himself, 'I shall create numerous Buddhist Kingdoms?' "[1] Subhuti replied, saying: "No! Honoured of the Worlds! And why? Because, kingdoms thus created would not in reality be Buddhist kingdoms, therefore 'the creation of numerous Buddhist kingdoms'[2] is merely a figure of speech."

The Lord Buddha, continuing, addressed Subhuti, saying: "Enlightened disciples ought therefore to engender within themselves a pure and holy mind; they ought not to depend on the phenomena of form, sound, odour, taste, touch or Law; they ought to sedulously cultivate a mind independent of every material aid."

The Lord Buddha addressed Subhuti, saying: "Supposing a man with a body as pretentious as Sumeru,[3] prince among mountains, would

---

[1] "Bhagavat said: If Subhuti, a Bodhisattva, should say, 'I shall create numbers of worlds,' he would say what is untrue. And why? Because, O subhuti, when Tathagata preached numbers of worlds, numbers of worlds indeed! They were preached by him as no numbers. Therefore they are called numbers of worlds." —*The Vagrakkhedika.* MAX MÜLLER

[2] A Buddhist kingdom has no outward manifestation; it is a pure and holy condition of mind — *Ch. Annotation.* Compare this statement attributed to Jesus Christ: "The kingdom of heaven *is within you.*"

[3] "Sumeru is probably Elburz, an isolated mountain of the Caucasus range, 18,000 feet in height, and surrounded by low ground." — *Chinese Buddhism.* EDKINS

you esteem such a body as being great?" Subhuti replied, saying: "Exceedingly great, Honoured of the Worlds! And why? Because, the Lord Buddha referred not to a physical body,[1] but to mental and spiritual concepts of bodies, in which sense a body may be regarded as really Great."

The Lord Buddha addressed Subhuti, saying:

> *"But when they brought the painted palanquin*
> *To fetch him home, the bearers of the poles*
> *Were for Regents of the Earth, come down*
> *From Mount Sumeru."* — *The light of Asia.* ARNOLD

[1] The modification which Buddhism introduced to the idea of transmigration was necessitated by the early Buddhist theories of the nature of sentient beings; according to which, man consists of a number of different properties or qualities. . . these are Material Qualities, Sensations, Abstract Ideas, Predispositions of Mind, and Mental Powers. . . The first group, Material Qualities, are like a mass of foam, that gradually forms, and then vanishes. The second group, the Sensations, are like a bubble dancing on the face of the water. The third group, Abstract Ideas, are like the uncertain mirage that appears in the sunshine. The fourth group, the mental and moral Predispositions, are like the plantain stalk, without firmness or solidity. And the last group, the Thoughts, are like a spectre or magical illusion. The body itself is constantly changing. . . Man is never the same for two consecutive moments." (Compare Rhys Davids' *Buddhism*, and Spence Hardy's *Manual*.)

"For instance, Subhuti, a man might have a body and a large body, so that his size should be a large as the king of mountains, Sumeru. Do you think then, O Subhuti, that his selfhood would be large? Subhuti said, Yes! His selfhood would be large. And why? Because, when the Tathagata preached selfhood, selfhood indeed! It was preached by him as no selfhood. Therefore it is called selfhood." — *The Vagrakkhedika* MAX MÜLLER

"If there were rivers Ganges as numerous as the sands of the Ganges, would the aggregate grains of sand[1] be of considerable number?" Subhuti replied, saying: "Of very considerable number, Honoured of the Worlds! The rivers Ganges alone would be innumerable, and much more innumerable would be the grains of sand."

The Lord Buddha thereupon addressed Subhuti, saying: "I have a truth to declare unto you! If a good disciple, whether man or woman, in the exercise of charity, were to bestow an abundance of the seven treasures[2] that is sufficient to fill as many boundless universes as there are grains of sand in innumerable rivers, would the cumulative merit of such a disciple be considerable?" Subhuti replied, saying: "Very considerable, Honoured of the Worlds!"

The Lord Buddha then declared unto Subhuti, "If a good disciple, whether man or woman, were with implicit faith to adhere

---

1 "   *Sarvanikchepa, by which you deal*
    With all the sands of Ganga, till we come
    To Anta-Kalpas, where the unit is
    The sands of ten score Gungas."
—*The Light of Asia.* ARNOLD

2 Gold, silver, aquamarine, crystal, white coral, ruby and emerald. "As much of the seven precious substances as would fill as many great chiliocoms as there are sands in all the rivers above described." —*Kin-Kong-King.* BEAL

to a stanza of this Scripture, and diligently explain it to others, the consequent merit would be relatively greater than the other."

The Lord Buddha, continuing, said unto Subhuti: "Wherever this Scripture is proclaimed, even though it were but a stanza comprising four lines, you should realise that that place will be sanctified by the presence of the whole realm of gods, men and terrestrial spirits,[1] who ought unitedly to worship,[2] as if before a sacred shrine of Buddha. But what encomium shall express the merits of a disciple who rigorously observes, and diligently studies,[3] the text of this Scripture?

---

1 Adopting Max Müller's rendering, in Chinese text are *Tien*, *Ren*, and *O-Siu-Lo* — heaven, or gods — men, and *Asurus*; the latter defined as *fei-tien* — not celestial spirits.

2 "Whatever spirits have come together here, either belonging to the earth or living in the air, let us worship the perfect Buddha, revered by gods and men.

"Whatever spirits have come together here, either belonging to the earth or living in the air, let us worship the perfect *Dhamma* (Law), revered by gods and men.

"Whatever spirits have come together here, either belonging to the earth or living in the air, let us worship the perfect *Sangha* (community of monks), revered by gods and men.
— *Dhammapada.* MAX MÜLLER

3 Earnestness is the path of immortality (Nirvana), thoughtlessness the path of death. Those who are in earnest do not die, those who are thoughtless are as if dead already."
— *Dhammapada.* MAX MÜLLER

Subhuti, you should realise that such a disciple will be endowed[1] with spiritual powers commensurate with initiation in the supreme, incomparable and most wonderful Law.[2] Whatever place constitutes a depository for the sacred Scripture, there also the Lord

---

1 "They, O Subhuti, will be endowed with the highest wonder (with what excites the highest wonder). And in that place, O Subhuti, there dwells the teacher (Sasa, often the name of Buddha), or one after another holding the place of the wise preceptor. (This may refer to a succession of teachers handing down the tradition one to another)." — *The Vagrakkhedika* MAX MÜLLER

"Subhuti, know that this man has acquired knowledge of the most excellent and desirable of all Laws; and if this place where this Sutra is recited be worthy of all honour as the place of Buddha himself, so also is this disciple honourable and worthy of the highest respect." — *Kin-Kong-King.* BEAL

2 "The praises of the *Bana* (Law) are a favourite subject with the native authors... The discourses of Buddha are as a divine charm to cure the poison of evil desire; a divine medicine to heal the disease of anger; a lamp in the midst of the darkness of ignorance; a fire, like that which burns at the end of a Kalpa, to destroy the evils of a repeated existence; a meridian sun to dry up the mud of covetousness; a great rain to quench the flame of sensuality; a thicket to block up the road that leads to the Narakas (place of the wicked); a ship in which to sail to the opposite shore of the ocean of existence; a collyrium for taking away the eye-film of heresy; a moon to bring out the night-blowing lotus of merit; a succession of trees bearing immortal fruit, placed here and there, by which the traveller may be enabled to cross the desert of existence; ... a straight highway by which to pass to the incomparable wisdom; a door of entrance to the eternal city of Nirvana; ... a treasury of the best things it is possible to attain; and a power by which may be appeased the sorrow of every sentient being." — *Eastern Monachism.* SPENCE HARDY

Buddha may be found, together with disciples worthy of reverence and honour."

Upon that occasion, Subhuti enquired of the Lord Buddha, saying: "Honoured of the Worlds! By what name shall this Scripture be known, that we may regard it with reverence?" The Lord Buddha replied, saying: "Subhuti, this Scripture shall be known as *The Diamond Sutra*,[1] 'The Transcendent Wisdom,' by means of which we reach 'The Other Shore.' By this name shall you reverently regard it! And why? Subhuti, what the Lord Buddha has declared as 'transcendent wisdom', by means of which we shall reach 'the other shore', is not essentially 'transcendent wisdom' — in its essence it transcends all wisdom."

The Lord Buddha addressed Subhuti, saying:[2] "What think you? Did the Lord

---

1 A Chinese annotator observes, that as the "diamond" excels all other precious gems in brilliance and indestructibility, so also the "wisdom" of this Sutra transcends and shall outlive all other knowledge known to philosophy.

2 "Then what do you think, O Subhuti, is there anything that was preached by the Tathagata? Subhuti said; Not indeed, O Bhagavat, there is nothing that was preached by the Tathagata." — *The Vagrakkhedika* MAX MÜLLER

It appears to be one of the distinctive features of primitive Buddhism, that its founder made provision for the utmost development of the human intellect, within the spheres of religion and philosophy. According to the text of *The Diamond Sutra*, the Lord Buddha evidently disclaims any suggestion

Buddha formulate a precise system of Law or doctrine?" Subhuti replied, saying: "Honoured of the Worlds! The Lord Buddha did not formulate a precise system of Law or doctrine."

The Lord Buddha addressed Subhuti, saying: "What think you? Within the myriad worlds which comprise this universe, are the atoms of dust numerous?"[1] Subhuti replied, saying: "Very numerous, Honoured of the Worlds!"

---

on his part to formulate a "precise system of Law or doctrine" corresponding to the idea of a *creed*.

1 "Matter is infinitely divisible."—*The World as Idea and Will*. SCHOPENHAUER

> "After me repeat
> Your numeration . . .
> By Pundarikas unto Padumas,
> Which last is how you count the utmost grains
> Of Hastagiri ground to finest dust."

— *The Light of Asia*. ARNOLD

"If the Buddha was not a materialist, in the sense of believing in the eternal existence of material atoms, neither would he in any sense be called a 'spiritualist,' of believer in the eternal existence of abstract spirit. With him, creation did not proceed from an omnipotent spirit or mind evolving phenomena out of itself by the exercise of will, nor from an external, self-existing, self-evolving germ of any kind. As to the existence in the universe of any spiritual substance which was not matter and was imperceptible to the senses, it could not be proved." — *Buddhism*. WILLIAMS

"Subhuti, all these countless particles of dust Tathagata declares are no real particles; it is but an empty name by which they are known. Tathagata that all these systems of worlds comprising the great chiliocosm are no real worlds; they are but empty names." — *Kin-Kong-King*. BEAL

The Lord Buddha continuing his discourse, said: "Subhuti, the Lord Buddha declares that all of these 'atoms of dust' are not essentially 'atoms of dust,' they are merely termed 'atoms of dust.' The Lord Buddha also declares that those 'myriad worlds' are not really 'myriad worlds,' they are merely designated 'myriad worlds.'"

The Lord Buddha addressed subhuti, saying: "What think you? Can the Lord Buddha be perceived by means of his thirty-two bodily distinctions?"[1] Subhuti replied, saying: "No!

---

1 "Characteristic physiological marks by which every Buddha may be recognised." — *Handbook of Chinese Buddhism*. EITEL

"Can Tathagata be known by the thirty-two signs (of a hero)?"
— *The Vagrakkhedika* MAX MÜLLER

> "The King saluted, and Queen Maya made
> To lay her babe before such holy feet;
> But when he saw the prince the old man cried
> 'Ah, Queen not so!' and thereupon he touched
> Eight times the dust, laid his waste visage there,
> Saying, 'O Babe! I worship! Thou art He!
> I see the rosy light, the foot sole marks,
> The soft-curled tendrils of the Swastika,
> The sacred primal signs thirty-and-two,
> The eighty lesser tokens. Thou art Buddha,
> And thou wilt preach the Law and save all flesh
> Who learn the Law."

— *The Light of Asia*. ARNOLD

"Bright were the divine lineaments of his face, and as that Master (of the Law) gazed in awe and holy reverence, he knew not how to compare the spectacle; the body of Buddha and his Kashaya robe were of a yellowish red colour, and from his knees upward the distinguishing marks of his person were exceedingly

Honoured of the Worlds! The Lord Buddha cannot be perceived by means of his thirty-two bodily distinctions. And why? Because, what the Lord Buddha referred to as his 'thirty-two bodily distinctions,' are not in reality 'bodily distinctions,' they are merely defined as 'bodily distinctions.' "

The Lord Buddha addressed Subhuti, saying: "If a good disciple, whether man or woman, day by day sacrificed lives innumerable as the sands of the Ganges;[1] and if another disciple adhered with implicit faith to a stanza of this Scripture, and diligently explained it to others, the intrinsic merit of such a disciple would be relatively greater than the other."[2]

Upon that occasion, the venerable Subhuti, hearing the text of this scripture proclaimed, and profoundly realising its meaning, was

---

glorious." — *The Light of Hiuen-Tsang.* BEAL

1 The Chinese expression *Shen-Ming* — life, invariably refers to life in an ordinary material sense, and which may be offered in sacrifice. But in Buddhist philosophy there is a spiritual *Atman*, which can be disposed of only by knowledge.

2 "Were anyone to fill the bowl of Buddha with the choicest food, or to present oil, sugar, honey, medicaments in the greatest abundance, or build thousands of *Wiharas* (monasteries or temples) splendid as those of Anuradhapura (an ancient city in Ceylon, the Anurogrammum of Ptolemy), or present an offering to Buddha like that of Anepidu (a rich merchant of Sewet), the hearing or reading of one stanza of the *Bana* (Law) would be more meritorious than all." - *Eastern Monachism.* HARDY

moved to tears. Addressing the Lord Buddha, he said: "Thou art of transcendent wisdom, Honoured of the Worlds! The Lord Buddha is expounding this supreme canon of Scripture, surpassing in perspicuity every exposition previously heard by me, since my eyes were privileged to perceive this most excellent wisdom.[1] Honoured of the Worlds! In years to some, if disciples, hearing this Scripture proclaimed, and having within their minds a pure and holy faith, engender true concepts engender true concepts of the ephemeral nature of phenomena — we ought to realise that the cumulative merit of such disciples will be intrinsic and wonderful. Honoured of the Worlds! The true concept of phenomena is, that these are not essentially phenomena, and hence the Lord Buddha declared that they are merely termed phenomena.

"Honoured of the Worlds! Having heard this unprecedented Scripture; faith, clear understanding, and firm resolve to observe its precepts, follow as a natural sequence. If, in future ages, disciples destined to hear

---

[1] "As one raises what has been overthrown, or reveals what has been hidden, or tells the way to him who has gone astray, or holds out an oil lamp in the dark that those who have eyes may see objects, even so by the venerable Gotama in manifold ways the *Dhamma* (Law) has been illustrated." — *Dhammapada*. MAX MÜLLER

this scripture, likewise believe, understand, and observe its precepts, their merit will incite the highest wonder and praise.[1] And why? Because, the minds of those disciples[2] will have outgrown such arbitrary ideas of phenomena as an entity, a being, a living being, or a personality. And why? Because, the entity is in reality a non-entity; and a being, a living being, or a personality, are ideas equally nebulous and hypothetical.[3] Wherefore, discarding every arbitrary idea of phenomena, the wise and wholly enlightened were severally designated Buddha."[4]

---

1 The chief of the priests of that establishment (the Jayendra convent) was a man of high moral character. He observed with the greatest strictness the religious rules and ordinances. He was possessed of the highest intelligence and acquainted with all the points of a true disciple. His talents were eminent; his spiritual powers exalted; and his disposition affectionate." — *The Life of Hiuen-Tsang*. BEAL

2 "They had within themselves the possession of a power by which all objective truth could be presented to their intellectual vision. They, therefore, partook of what in other systems would be regarded as divinity." — *Eastern Monarchism*. HARDY

3 "They are divided into existing and non-existing; real and unreal, by those with wrong notions; other laws also, of permanency, of being produced from something already produced, are wrongly assumed." - *Saddharma-Pandarika*. KERN

4 "But, O Bhagavad, there will not arise in them any idea of a self, or a being, of a living being, of a person, nor does there exist for them any idea of no-idea. And why? Because the idea of self is a no-idea, the idea of a being is a no-idea, the idea of a living being is a no-idea, the idea of a person is a no-idea. And why? Because, the blessed Buddhas are freed from all ideas." — *The Vagrakkhedika* MAX MÜLLER

The Lord Buddha, assenting, said unto Subhuti: "If, in future ages, disciples destined to hear this Scripture, neither become perturbed by its extreme modes of thought,[1] nor alarmed buy its lofty sentiments,[2] nor apprehensive about realising its high ideals[3] — these disciples also, by their intrinsic merit, will incite superlative wonder and praise.

"Subhuti, what the Lord Buddha referred to as the first *Paramita*[4] (charity), is not in reality the first Paramita, it is merely termed the first Paramita.

"Subhuti, regarding the third Paramita (endurance), it is not in reality a Paramita, it is mere termed a Paramita. And why?

---

1 ... *"For birth and death*
 End hence for me and those who learn my Law."
— *The Light of Asia.* ARNOLD

2 "As the Buddhist strove to reach a state of quietism or holy meditation in this world, namely the state of the perfect disciple or Arhat; so he looked forward to an eternal calm in Nirvana, the world to come. Buddha taught that this end could only be attained by the practice of virtue. — T*he Indian Empire.* HUNTER

3 *"The heart of it is love, the end of it*
 Is peace and consummation sweet."

— *The Light of Asia.* ARNOLD

4 The first of six *Paramita* — charity, morality, endurance, energy, contemplation, wisdom; or means of attaining to Nirvana.

"What the Tathagata preaches as the *Prajna-Paramita*, that was preached also by innumerable Blessed Buddhas. Therefore it is called the *Parjma-Paramita*." — *The Vagrakkhedika* MAX MÜLLER

Because, in a previous life, when the Prince of Kalinga¹ ("Kaliradja") severed the flesh from my limbs and body, at that time I was oblivious to such arbitrary ideas of phenomena as an entity, a being, a living being, or a personality. And why? Because, upon that occasion, when my limbs and body were rent asunder, had I not been oblivious to such arbitrary ideas an entity, a being, a living being, or a personality, there would have originated within my mind, feelings of anger and resentment.

"Subhuti, five hundred incarnations ago,²

---

1 "An ancient kingdom S.E. of Kos'ala, a nursery of heretical sects, the present Calingapatah, a town in the northern Circars (Lat, 18°15 N., Long. 85° 11 E.) — *Handbook of Chinese Buddhism.* EITEL

It is recorded the Lord Buddha, in a previous incarnation, was living in a mountainous region, strictly observing the monastic vows. The Prince of Kalinga, a cruel and dissolute ruler, having organised a hunting expedition, visited the secluded region, accompanied by numerous ladies of his harem. Fatigued by the excitement of the chase, the prince fell into a deep siesta. Meantime, the ladies resolved upon a short excursion along a mountain path. Unexpectedly meeting the Lord Buddha, they were greatly astonished at his dignified bearing and edifying conversation. When the prince awoke from his siesta, he was irritated to find that his ladies had disappeared. Instituting an immediate search, he became filled with implacable rage upon discovering them in the society of a hermit. The incident, as narrated in the Chinese text, proved to be a distressing sequel to the modest ladies' innocent adventure. (Compare *Chinese Annotations,* etc.)

2 "Various forms of pre-existence to the number of 500 or 550 are recorded, in the course of which he (Buddha)

I recollect that as a recluse practising the ordinances of the Kshanti-Paramita,[1] even then I had no such arbitrary ideas as an entity, a being, a living being, or a personality. Therefore, Subhuti, an enlightened disciple ought to disregard as unreal and illusive, every conceivable form of phenomena.[2] In aspiring to supreme spiritual wisdom, the mind ought to be insensible to every sensuous

---

marked his way up through as many stages of transmigration from the lowest spheres of life to the highest, practising all kinds of asceticism, and exhibiting in every form the utmost unselfishness and charity." — *Handbook of Chinese Buddhism*. EITEL

"I and thou, O Arjuna! have passed through many transmigrations. I know all these... Even though I am unborn, of changeless essence, and the lord also of all which exist, yet, in presiding over nature (Prakrita), which is mine, I am born by my own mystic power (Maya). For whenever there is a relaxation of duty ... and an increase of impiety, I then reproduce myself for the protection of the good ... I am produced in every age." — *Ghagavad-Gita*. THOMSON

1 "Explained by patient endurance of insult. The virtue of patience, implying constant equanimity under persecution, and excluding hatred and revenge." — *Handbook of Chinese Buddhism*. EITEL

"Because, O Subhuti, I remember the past five hundred births, when I was the *Rishi-Kshantivadin* (preacher of endurance)." — *The Vagrakkhedika*. MAX MÜLLER

2 "Let (the Bodhisattva) be concentrated in mind, attentive, ever firm as the peak of Mount Sumeru, and in such a state (of mind) look upon all laws (and things) as having the nature of space (as being void), permanently equal to space, without essence, immovable, without substantiality. These, indeed, are the Laws, all and for ever." — *Suddharma-Pundarika*. KERN

influence, and independent of everything pertaining to sound, odour, taste, touch or Law. There ought to be cultivated a condition of complete independence of mind; because, if the mind is depending on any external aid, it is obviously deluded — there is in reality nothing external to depend upon.[1] Therefore, the Lord Buddha declared that in the exercise of charity, the mind of an enlightened disciple ought not to depend upon any form of phenomena. Subhuti, an enlightened disciple desirous to confer benefits upon the whole realm of being, ought thus to be animated in the exercise of charity.[2]

"The Lord Buddha, in declaring the 'unreality of phenomena,' also affirmed 'that whole realm of sentient life is ephemeral and illusory.'[3]

"Subhuti, the sayings of the Lord Buddha are true, credible and immutable. His

---

[1] "Because what is believed is not believed (is not to be depended on). — *The Vagrakkhedika.* MAX MÜLLER

[2] "Hence Buddha declares that the mind of a Bodhisatwa ought not to rely on any formal act of charity. Subhuti, the Bodhisatwa ought to distribute his almsgiving for the purpose of benefiting the whole mass of sentient creatures, and yet Tathagata declares that as all dependencies are after all no real subjects of dependence, so also he says that all sentient creatures are not in reality what they are called." — *Kin-Kong-King.* BEAL

[3] Literally translated, "Every form of phenomena is really *not* phenomena; sentient life is in reality *not* sentient life."

utterances are neither extravagant nor chimerical. Subhuti, the plane of thought[1] to which the Lord Buddha attained, cannot be explained in terms synonymous with reality or non-reality.

"Subhuti, in the exercise of charity, if the mind of an enlightened disciple is not independent of every Law, he is like unto a person having entered impenetrable darkness, and to whom every object is invisible. But an enlightened disciple, discharging the exercise of charity with a mind independent of every Law, is like unto a person having the power of vision, in the meridian glory of the sunlight, and to whom every object is visible.

"Subhuti, in future ages, if a good disciple, whether man or woman, rigorously studies and observes the text of the Scripture: the Lord Buddha, by means of his Buddhic wisdom,[2]

---

1 The Buddhist term, *Fah* (Law).

2 "The omniscience of Buddha is not the knowledge of all things, but the power of knowing whatever he wishes to know. In opposition to other teachers, who deduce their doctrines from certain previously assumed principles, and who may err either in the data, or in the deductions from them. Buddha affirms of himself that the complete field of truth is before him, that the eye of wisdom to perceive it was obtained by him when he became a Buddha; and wherever he desires to know he perceives perfectly, and at one glance, without any reasoning process."
— Rev. D. Gogerly in the *Ceylon Friend*, quoted in *Eastern Monachism*. HARDY

entirely knows and perceives that for such a disciple there is reserved a cumulative merit, immeasurable and illimitable."

The Lord Buddha addressed Subhuti, saying: "If a good disciple, whether man or woman, in the morning, at noonday and at eventide, sacrificed lives innumerable as the sands of the Ganges, and thus without intermission throughout infinite ages; and if another disciple, hearing this Scripture proclaimed, steadfastly believed it, his felicity would be appreciably greater than the other. But how much greater must be the felicity of a disciple who transcribes the sacred text, observes its precepts, studies its Laws, and repeats the Scripture that others might be edified thereby?

"Subhuti, the relevant importance of this Scripture may thus be summarily stayed; its truth is infinite; its worth incomparable; and its merit interminable.

"The Lord Buddha delivered this Scripture specifically for those who are entered upon the path which leads to Nirvana, and for those who are attaining to the ultimate plane of Buddhic thought.[1] If a disciple rigorously

---

1 Literally, for the *ta-cheng-che* — those of the great vehicle, i.e. the Mahayana faith. "They (the Mahayana school) taught

observes, studies and widely disseminates the knowledge of this Scripture, the Lord Buddha entirely knows and perceives that for such an one there will be cumulative merit, immeasurable, incomparable, illimitable and inconceivable. All such disciples will be endowed with transcendent Buddha wisdom and enlightenment.[1] And why? Because, Subhuti, if a disciple takes pleasure in a narrow or exclusive form of the Law,[2] he cannot

---

that there were two methods of salvation, or, so to speak, two ways or two vehicles — the great and the little (Maha-Yana and Hina-Yana) — and indeed two Bodhis or forms of true knowledge which these vehicles had to convey (there was also a middle way) The former was for ordinary persons, the latter for beings of larger talents and higher spinritual powers." *Buddhism.* WILLIAMS

"Therefore let one always be thoughtful, and avoid (gross) pleasures; having abandoned them, let him cross the stream, after baling out the ship, and go to the other shore (Nirvana)." — *Dhammapada.* MAX MÜLLER

1 "All these beings will equally remember the *Bodhi* (the highest Buddhic knowledge), will receive it and understand it." — *The Vagrakkhedika.* MAX MÜLLER

"All men being one with *ho-tan* (Gautama?) Tathagata, arrive at the state of the unsurpassed, just and enlightened (Heart)." — *Kin-Kong-King.* BEAL

The Chinese phrase '*ho-tan-Ju-Lai,*' may mean to bear upon the person evidences of the Lord Buddha. Compare the statement of the apostle Paul, "I bear in my body evidences of the Lord Jesus Christ."

2 Those disciples associated with the *Siao-Fah* (little Law, the Hinayana school of Buddhist thought) are rather ungraciously referred to by a Chinese commentator as "rootless stems"; by which we are reminded of the Hindu aphorism, "from the

receive with gratification[1] the instruction of this Scripture, or delight in its study, or fervently explain it to others. Subhuti, in whatever place there is a repository for this Scripture, the whole realm of spiritual beings ought to adore it; and reverencing it as a sacred shrine,[2] ceremoniously surround it, scattering profusely sweet-scented flowers, and pure odours of fragrant incense."[3]

---

absence of a root within the root, all things are rootless."

1 When the Lord Buddha delivered the Sutra known as the *Lotus of the Good Law*, it is recorded that five thousand followers forsook him, owing to what they regarded as a grave difficulty in complying with its intensely abstruse doctrines.

2 "In these two places also Topes (where relics of Buddha are deposited and safeguarded) have been built, both adorned with layers of all the precious substances (gold, silver, pearls, coral, carnelian, glass and crystal). The kings, ministers and peoples of the kingdoms vie with one another in making offerings at them. The trains of those who come to scatter flowers and light lamps at them never cease." — *The Travels of Fa-Hien*. LEGGE

This descriptive scene concerning the endless trains of pilgrims who lit their lamps at the sacred shrine, may recall to our minds the beautifully expressed line in Sophocles' *Œdipus Coloneus,* thus rendered by Professor Jebb, *The torch-lit strand of Eleusis.*

3 Then the king, with his assembled ministers and all the priests belonging to their capital (of Kasmir), advanced to the preaching hall (*Dharmasala*), and escorted him (the Master of the Law) onwards, being altogether something like a thousand men, with standards and parasols, with incense and flowers filling the roads. When they met (the Master if the Law) they all performed a humble salutation, and spread before him countless flowers as religious offerings." — *The Life of Hiuen-Tsang*. BEAL

The Lord Buddha, continuing, addressed Subhuti, saying: "If a good disciple, whether man or woman, devoted to the observance and study of this Scripture, is thereby despised, or lightly esteemed,[1] it is because that in a previous life there had been committed some grievous transgression, followed now by inexorable retribution.[2] But, although in this life despised or highly esteemed, the compensating merit thus acquired will cause the transgression of a former life to be fully expiated, and the disciple adequately recompensed by the attainment of supreme spiritual wisdom.

"Furthermore, Subhuti, numberless ages ago, I recollect that before the advent of Dipankara Buddha, there were myriad Buddhas before whom I served and received

---

1 "Whoever reviles Buddha or his disciple, be he a wandering midcoast, or a householder, let one know him as an outcast. — *Sutta-Nipata*. FAUSBÖLL

2 "Whatever evil deeds those beings have done in a former birth, deeds must lead to suffering, those deeds these beings, owing to their being overcome, after they have seen the Law, will destroy, and they will obtain the knowledge of Buddha." — *The Vagrakkhedika*. MAX MÜLLER

"According to the Buddha... all men must suffer in their own persons in the present life, or in future lives, the consequences of their own acts... The penalty of sin could not be transferred to another — it could only be borne by the sinner himself, just as the reward of virtue could only be enjoyed by the virtuous man himself." — *Hinduism*. WILLIAMS

religious instruction, my conduct being entirely blameless and without reproach. But, in the ages to come, if a disciple be enabled to rigorously observe and to study the text of this Scripture, the merit thus acquired will so far exceed the measure of my merit in the service of this myriad Buddhas, that it cannot be stated in terms of proportion, nor comprehended by means of any 'analogy.'

"Again, Subhuti, in future ages, if a good disciple, whether man or woman, is enabled to rigorously observe and to study consecutively the texts of this Scripture, were I to elaborate the nature or extent of this, meritless who heard it might become delirious, or entirely doubt its credibility.[1] Subhuti, it is necessary to realise, that as the meaning of this scripture is beyond ordinary comprehension, the scope of its fruitful rewards is equally incomprehensible."[2]

Upon that occasion, the venerable Subhuti addressed the Lord Buddha, saying: "Honoured of the Worlds! If a good disciple,

---

[1] Literal translation, "become as doubtful as a fox."

[2] "For the method and entire meaning of this Sutra is not to be described or entirely conceived, so the merit and happy consequences of accepting it cannot be conceived or described." — *Kin-Kong-King*. BEAL

whether man or woman, having desired to attain to supreme spiritual wisdom, what immutable Law shall support the mind of that disciple, and bring into submission every inordinate desire?" [1]

The Lord Buddha replied, saying: "A good disciple, whether man or woman, ought thus to habituate his mind: [2] 'I must become oblivious to every idea of sentient life, and having become oblivious to every idea of sentient life, there is *no one* to whom the idea of sentient life has become oblivious,' [3] And

---

1 "Let a man restraining all these remain in devotion . . . For he, whose senses are under his control, possesses spiritual knowledge. Attachments to objects of sense arise in a man who meditates upon them; from attachment springs desire; from desire, passion springs up; from passion comes bewilderment; from bewilderment, confusion of the memory; destruction of the intellect; from destruction of the intellect, he perishes."
— *Bhagavad-Gita*. Cockburn Thomson

2 "He should thus frame his thought: all things must be delivered by me in the perfect world of Nirvana . . . And why? Because, O Subhuti, there is no such thing as one who has entered on the path of the Bodhisattva." — *The Vagrakkhedika*. Max Müller

3 "Such scenes as the following, illustrating the beliefs of the time and the locality, would not seldom occur. A wayfarer in the country of the Getae (Jats) (Afghanistan) knocks at the door of a Brahman family. A young man within answers: 'There is No One in this house.' The traveller was too well taught in Buddhism not to know the meaning of this philosophical nihilism, and at once answered, 'Who is No One?' The young man, when he heard this, felt that he was understood. A kindred spirit was outside. He opened the door and allowed the stranger to enter. The visitor was the patriarch of the time (seventeenth), with staff and

why? Because, Subhuti, if an enlightened disciple retains within his mind such arbitrary ideas of sentient life as an entity, a being, a living being, or a personality, he has not attained to supreme spiritual wisdom. And why? Because, Subhuti, there is no Law by means of which a disciple may be defined as having attained supreme spiritual wisdom." [1]

---

rice bowl, travelling to teach and make new disciples." — *Chinese Buddhism.* EDKINS

[1] Most writers of the Buddhist faith and religion refer to the series of events which culminated in the Siddhārtha or Gautama Buddha obtaining "supreme enlightenment." The founder of the Buddhist faith, dissatisfied with the practice of asceticism, and disappointed by his unfaithful disciples, walked meditatively toward the river Nairanjara, where Sujata, "the daughter of a neighbouring villager," provided him with his morning meal. Seating himself under a sacred Bo-Tree, immediately he became engaged in the severest of mental conflicts. The Buddhist authors describe their Master as sitting "sublime," "calm," and "serene" throughout the sustained assault of a 'visible" and wicked tempter, assisted by legions of evil spirits. So unrelenting was the fierce encounter, that the forces of nature shook and were convulsed under the dreadful onslaught. As the day advanced, the spiritual elements in Buddha's nature gradually gained the ascendency; and when he became "fully enlightened," there was revealed to him an antidote for human woe. The mind of the Lord Buddha thereafter assumed an aspect of perfect peace; and in "*the power over the human heart of inward culture, and of love to others,*" the great Teacher discovered a foundation of Truth, where, with assurance of faith, he could securely rest. As Milton regarded "Paradise" to be "regained" in the wilderness, in like manner, the Buddhist poets indicate a belief that the experience of their Master under the Bo-Tree was the most eventful in his history. That is why they regard the Bo-Tree with a reverence resembling the Christian veneration of the Cross. (Compare Davids' *Buddhism*.)

The Lord Buddha addressed Subhuti, saying: "What think you? When the Lord Buddha was a disciple of Dipankara Buddha, was there bequeathed to him any Law whereby he attained to supreme spiritual wisdom?" Subhuti replied, saying: "No, Honoured of the Worlds! Inasmuch as I am able to comprehend the meaning of the Lord Buddha's discourse, when the Lord Buddha was a disciple of Dipankara Buddha, there was no law bequeathed to him whereby he attained to supreme spiritual wisdom."

The Lord Buddha endorsed these words, saying:[1] "Truly there is no Law by means of which the Lord Buddha obtained supreme spiritual wisdom. Subhuti, if there existed a Law by means of which the Lord Buddha obtained spiritual wisdom, Dipankara Buddha would not have foretold at my initiation, 'In future ages,[2] thou shalt become Sakyamuni

---

1 Buddha said "Right! Right! Subhuti, there is in truth no fixed Law (by which) Tathagata attained this condition. Subhuti, if there had been such a Law, then Dipankara Buddha would not have said in delivering the prediction concerning me: 'You in after ages must attain to the state of Buddha, and your name shall be Sakyamuni.' so that because there is indeed no fixed Law for attaining the condition of 'the perfect heart,' on that account it was Dipankara Buddha delivered his prediction in such words." — *Kin-Kong-King.* BEAL

2 "To the pious Buddhist it is a constant source of joy and gratitude that 'the Buddha,' not only then, but in many former births, when emancipation from all cares and troubles of life

Buddha.' But, in reality, there is no Law by means of which supreme spiritual wisdom can be attained. Therefore, at my initiation, Dipankara Buddha foretold concerning me, 'In future ages, thou shalt become Sakyamuni Buddha.' And why? Because, in the word *Buddha*,[1] every Law is summarily and intelligibly comprehended.

"If a disciple affirmed that the Lord Buddha attained to supreme spiritual wisdom, it is necessary to state that there is no Law whereby this condition of mind can be realised. The supreme spiritual wisdom to which the Lord Buddha attained cannot, in its essence, be defined as real or unreal. Thus, the Lord

---

was within his reach, should again and again, in mere love for man, have condescended to enter the world, and live amidst the sorrows inseparable from finite existence." — *Buddhism*. RHYS DAVIDS

1 "And why, O Subhuti, the name of Tathagata? It expresses 'true suchness.' And why Tathagata, O Subhuti? It expresses that 'he had no origin.' And why Tathagata, O Subhuti? It expresses 'the destruction of all qualities'. And why Tathagata, O Subhuti? It expresses 'one who has no origin whatever.' And why this? Because, O Subhuti, 'no origin is the highest goal.'" — *The Vagrakkhedika*. MAX MÜLLER

The familiar word *Buddha* seems to convey to devout Buddhists a meaning consonant with the ethical idea of *Love*, as generally understood by Christians. Within it are potential spiritual elements, which, to Christians, perfectly fulfil the Law. The Chinese text, *Ju-Lai-che, chi-chu-fah-ru-i*, may bear the following interpretation, "*Buddha is the One in whom all Laws become intelligible.*"

Buddha declared that the ordinarily accepted term 'the Buddha Law,' is synonymous with every moral and spiritual Law. Subhuti, what are ordinarily declared to be 'systems of Law,' are not in reality 'systems of Law,' they are merely terms 'systems of Law.'"

The Lord Buddha enquired of Subhuti, saying: "Can you imagine a man having a great physical body?" Subhuti replied, saying: "The Lord Buddha, discoursing upon the proportions of a physical body, did not maintain for these any real greatness, therefore it is merely termed 'a great body.'"

The Lord Buddha, thereupon, addressed Subhuti, saying: "Thus it is with an enlightened disciple: if he were to expiate after this manner, 'I must become oblivious to every idea of sentient life,[1] he could not

---

1 "And if a Bodhisattva were to say: 'I shall deliver all beings,' he ought not to be called a Bodhisattva. And why? Is there anything, O Subhuti, that is called a Bodhisattva? Subhuti said: 'Not indeed!' Bhagavad said; "Those who were spoken of as beings, beings indeed, O Subhuti, they were spoken of as no-beings by the Tathagata, and therefore they are called beings. Therefore Tathagata says: 'All beings are without self, all beings are without life, without manhood, without personality.'" — *The Vagrakkhedika.* MAX MÜLLER

"Subhuti, so it is with the Bohisattwa, if he should say: 'I ought to destroy all recollection of the countless kinds of creatures,' this Bodhsiatwa would not be really one, but only a nominal one . . . Hence Buddha says that all things ought to be without individual distinction." — *Kin-Kong-King.* BEAL

be described as fully enlightened. And why? Because, there is no Law whereby a disciple can be approved as 'fully enlightened.'[1] Therefore, the Lord Buddha declared that within the realm of spiritual Law, there is neither an entity, a being, a living being, nor a personality."

The Lord Buddha addressed Subhuti, saying: "If an enlightened disciple were to speak in this wise, 'I shall create numerous Buddhist kingdoms,' he could not be designated 'fully enlightened.' And why? Because, the Lord Buddha, discoursing upon 'creating numerous Buddhist kingdoms,' did not affirm the idea of creating numerous 'material' Buddhist kingdoms, hence the 'creation of numerous Buddhist kingdoms' is merely a figure of speech. Subhuti, the Lord Buddha has declared that a disciple may be regarded as 'truly enlightened,' whose mind is thoroughly imbued with the Law of non-individuality."[2]

---

[1] "The fountain of knowledge is the pure, bright, self-enlightened mind." — *Twan-Tsi-Sin-Yao* (Tang Dynasty). Compare *Chinese Buddhism*, by Edkins.

[2] "A Bodhisattva, O Subhuti, who believes that all things are without self, he has faith, he is called a noble-minded Bodhisattva by the holy and enlightened Tathagata." — *The Vagrakkhedika*. MAX MÜLLER

In the *Mo-Wei-Sutra*, the ordinary concepts of an entity, a being, a living being, or a personality, are referred to as *blots* or

The Lord Buddha enquired of Subhuti, saying: "What think you Subhuti? Does the Lord Buddha possess the physical eye?" Subhuti assented saying: "Honoured of the Worlds! The Lord Buddha truly possesses the physical eye."

The Lord Buddha enquired again of Subhuti, saying: "What think you? Does the Lord Buddha possess the divine or spiritual eye?" Subhuti assented, saying, "Honoured of the Worlds! The Lord Buddha truly possesses the divine or spiritual eye."

The Lord Buddha then enquired of Subhuti, saying: "What think you? Does the Lord Buddha possess the eye of wisdom?" Subhuti assented, saying: "Honoured of the Worlds! The Lord Buddha truly possesses the eye of wisdom."

The Lord Buddha enquired of Subhuti, saying: "What think you, does the Lord Buddha possess the eye of truth?" Subhuti assented, saying: "Honoured of the Worlds! The Lord Buddha truly possesses the eye of truth."[1]

---

stains
upon the mind.

[1] The Chinese *Fah-Yen*—literally, Eye of the Law.

The Lord Buddha enquired of Subhuti: "What think you? Does the Lord Buddha possess the Buddhic eye?" Subhuti assented, saying: "Honoured of the Worlds! The Lord Buddha truly possesses the Buddhic eye."[1]

The Lord Buddha enquired of Subhuti, saying: "What think you? Concerning the sands of the Ganges, did the Lord Buddha declare that these were grains of sand?" Subhuti assented, saying: "Honoured of the Worlds! The Lord Buddha declared that these were grains of sand."

The Lord Buddha enquired of Subhuti, saying: "What think you? If there were as many rivers Ganges as there are grains of sand in the Ganges, and if there were

---

"The second of three great treasures is called *Dhammo*, or in Singalese, *Dharmma*. This word has various meanings, but is here to be understood in the sense of Truth. It is not infrequently translated 'the Law,' but this interpretation gives an idea contrary to the entire genius of Buddhism. The *Dharmma* is therefore emphatically the Truth." — E*astern Monarchism.* SPENCE HARDY

1 "Supernatural talents, which the founder of Buddhism, Sakyamuni, is believed to have acquired in the night before he became Buddha, and which every Arhat takes possession of by means of the fourth degree of *Dhyana* (abstract contemplation). Most Chinese texts reckon six such talents, while the Sinhalese know only five. Sometimes, however, only five are mentioned." — *Handbook of Chinese Buddhism.* EITEL

The physical eye has an ordinary local function. The divine or spiritual eye has a universal function. The eye of wisdom is affiliated with the Law, and attests its immutability. The Buddha eye is the instrument of salvation.— *Chinese Annotation.*

as many Buddhist worlds as the grains of sand in these innumerable rivers, would these Buddhist worlds be numerous?" Subhuti replied, saying: "Honoured of the Worlds! These Buddhist worlds would be very numerous."

The Lord Buddha, continuing, addressed Subhuti, saying: "Within these innumerable worlds, every form of sentient life, with their various mental dispositions, are entirely known to the Lord Buddha.[1] And why? Because, what the Lord Buddha referred to as 'various mental dispositions,' are not in reality 'various mental dispositions,' these are merely termed their 'various mental dispositions.' And why? Because, Subhuti, dispositions of mind, or modes of thought,

---

1 "Bhagavad said, as many beings as there would be in all those worlds, I know the manifold trains of thought of them all. And why? Because, what was preached as the trains of thought, the trains of thought indeed, O Subhuti, that was preached by Tathagata as no-train of thoughts. And why? Because, O Subhuti, a past thought is not perceived, a future thought is not perceived, and the present thought is not perceived. — *The Vagrakkhedika*. MAX MÜLLER

"Gautama himself was very early regarded as omniscient, and absolutely sinless. His perfect wisdom is declared by the ancient epithet of *Samma-Sambuddha*, 'the completely enlightened one,' found at the commencement of every Pali text; and at the present day in Ceylon, the usual way in which Gautama is styled is *Sarwajnan-Wahanse*, 'the venerable omniscient one.' From his perfect wisdom, according to Buddhist belief, his sinlessness would follow as a matter of course." — *Buddhism*. RHYS DAVIDS

whether relating the past, the present, or the future, are alike, unreal and illusory."

The Lord Buddha addressed Subhuti, saying: "What think you? If a disciple, having obtained all the treasures of this universe,[1] were to bestow these in the exercise of charity, would such a disciple enjoy a considerable merit?" Subhuti, assenting, said: "Honoured of the Worlds! Such a disciple would consequently enjoy a very considerable merit."[2]

The Lord Buddha thereupon addressed Subhuti, saying: "If there were any real or permanent quality in merit, then Lord Buddha would not have spoken of such merit as 'considerable.' It is because there is neither a tangible nor material quality in merit, that the Lord Buddha referred to the merit of that

---

1 The seven treasures — gold, silver, aquamarine, crystal, white coral, ruby and emerald.

2 "Because, what was preached as a stock of merit, a stock of merit indeed, O Subhuti, that was preached as no-stock of merit by the Tathagata, and therefore it is called a stock of merit. If, O Subhuti, there existed a stock of merit, Tathagata would not have preached a stock of merit, a stock of merit indeed!" — *The Vagrakkhedika.* MAX MÜLLER

Within the meaning of the Buddhic Law, charity is purely a spiritual concept; merit consequent upon fulfilling the Law of charity must have a purely spiritual realisation. This is the sense in which the Lord Buddha referred to merit as "considerable." — *Chinese Annotation.*

disciple as 'considerable.'"

The Lord Buddha addressed Subhuti, saying: "What think you? Can the Lord Buddha be perceived my means of his perfect material body?"[1] Subhuti replied, saying: "Honoured of the Worlds! It is improbable that the Lord Buddha can be perceived by means of his perfect material body. And why? Because, what the Lord Buddha referred to as a 'perfect material body,' is not in reality a 'perfect material body,' it is merely termed a 'perfect material body.'"

The Lord Buddha addressed Subhuti, saying: "What think you? Can the Lord Buddha be perceived by means of any physical

---

1 "The first of the Buddha's bodies is the *Dharma-Kaya* (body of the Law), supposed to be a kind of ethereal essence of a sublimated nature and co-extensive with space. The essence was believed to be eternal, and after the Buddha's death, was represented by the Law or doctrine (*Dharma*) he taught.

"The second body is the *Sambhoga-Kaya*, 'body of conscious bliss,' which is of a less ethereal and more material nature than the last. Its Brahmanical analogue appears to be the intermediate body (belonging to departed spirits) called *Bhoga-Deha*, which is of an ethereal character, though composed of sufficiently gross (*Sthula*) material particles to be capable of experiencing happiness or misery.

"The third body is the *Nirmana-Kaya*, 'body of visible shapes and transformations,' that is to say, those various concrete material forms in which every Buddha who exists as an invisible and eternal essence, is manifested on the earth or elsewhere for the propagation of the true doctrine." — *Buddhism*. WILLIAMS

THE DIAMOND SUTRA

phenomena?"[1] Subhuti replied, saying: "Honoured of the Worlds! It is improbable that the Lord Buddha can be perceived by means of any physical phenomena. And why? Because, what the Lord Buddha referred to as 'physical phenomena,' are not in reality 'physical phenomena,' these are merely termed 'physical phenomena.'"

The Lord Buddha addressed Subhuti, saying: "Do not affirm that the Lord Buddha thinks this within himself, 'I ought to promulgate a system of Law or doctrine.' Have no such irrelevant thought! And why? Because, if a disciple affirmed that the Lord Buddha promulgated a system of Law or doctrine, he would defame the Lord Buddha, being manifestly unable to understand the purport of my instruction. Subhuti, regarding

---

[1] "What think you, O Subhuti, is a Tathagata to be seen (known) by the shape of his visible body? Subhuti said, not indeed, a tathagata is not to be seen (known) by the shape of his visible body. And why? Because, what was preached as the shape of the visible body, the shape of the visible body indeed, that was preached by Tathagata as no-shape of the visible body, and therefore it is called the shape of the visible body." — *The Vagrakkhedika.* MAX MÜLLER

Herein is exemplification of the surpassing excellence of spiritual phenomena: although outwardly possessed of the thirty-two primal signs of a Buddha, there were also the essential evidences of those marvellous physical perfections which constitute the *real* Buddha —
Chinese Annotation.

the promulgation of a 'system of Law or doctrine,' there is in reality no 'system of Law or doctrine' to promulgate, it is merely termed a 'system of Law or doctrine.'"[1]

Upon that occasion, the virtuous and venerable Subhuti enquired of the Lord Buddha, saying: "Honoured of the Worlds! In ages to come, will sentient beings destined to hear this Law,[2] engender within their minds the essential elements of faith?" The Lord Buddha replied, saying: "Subhuti, it cannot be asserted that these are sentient beings, or that these are not sentient beings. And why? Because, Subhuti, regarding 'sentient beings,' the Lord Buddha declared that in reality

---

1 "Bhagavad said : What do you think, O Subhuti, does Tathagata think in this wise : the Law has been taught by me? Subhuti said : Not indeed O Bhagavad, does the Tathagata think in this wise : the Law has been taught by me. Bhagavad said : If a man should say that the Law has been taught by the Tathagata, he would say what is not true ; he would slander me with untruth which he has learned. And why? Because, O Subhuti, it is said the teaching of the Law, the teaching of the Law indeed, O Subhuti, there is nothing that can be perceived by the name of the teaching of the Law." — *The Vagrakkhedika.* MAX MÜLLER

Eminent wisdom possesses the natural beauty of a pellucid stream flowing swiftly between mountain crags; but a mind at rest from systems of Law or doctrine' is reminiscent of the loveliness of a waterfall, frozen into shining icicles, and resplendent in the light of the moon. — *Chinese Annotation*

2 "He is the best of all guides of men, no other being is like unto him; he is like a jewel of imperishable glory, who hears this Law with a pure heart." *The Buddha-Karita.* COWELL

these are not 'sentient beings,' they are merely termed 'sentient beings.' " [1]

Subhuti enquired of the Lord Buddha, saying: "Honoured of the Worlds! Did the Lord Buddha, in attaining to supreme spiritual wisdom, obtain nothing of a real or tangible nature?" The Lord Buddha replied, saying: "In attaining to supreme spiritual wisdom, not a vestige of Law or doctrine was obtained,[2] and therefore it is termed 'supreme spiritual wisdom.' "

The Lord Buddha addressed Subhuti,

---

1 "Bhagavad said: "These, O Subhuti, are neither beings nor no-beings. And why? Because, O Subhuti, those who were preached as beings, beings indeed, they were preached as no-beings by the Tathagata, and therefore they are called beings." — *The Vagrakkhedika.* MAX MÜLLER

Although these are ordinarily referred to as sentient beings, there are spiritual elements in their real natures, which place them in a category only imperfectly described by the term "sentient beings"; but possessing also evident material qualities, it might be an error to assert that these are not "sentient beings'; hence the declaration by the Lord Buddha "they are merely termed sentient beings." — *Chinese Annotation.*

2 "To affirm the existence of anything real or tangible in the nature of the Law, would be tantamount to being firmly bound by the Law; but to affirm that 'not even a vestige of Law or doctrine was obtained,' is the equivalent of being absolutely free from the Law." –*Yen-Ping* (a Chinese monk).

"Buddha said; 'True, true, Subhuti! I, as possessed of this heart, have come into the condition above described. This term, the unsurpassed, just and enlightened heart, is but a mere name." —*Kin-Kong-King.* BEAL saying: "This Law is coherent and indivisible,[1] it is neither 'above' nor 'below,'[2] therefore it is termed 'supreme spiritual wisdom.' It excludes such arbitrary ideas as an entity, a being, a living being, or a personality; but includes every Law pertaining the cultivation of goodness.[3] Subhuti, what were referred to as 'Laws pertaining to goodness,' these the Lord Buddha declared are not in reality 'Laws pertaining to goodness,'

---

1 The Abbé Dubois in his valuable book, *Hindu Manners, Customs and Ceremonies*, carefully observes that amongst the attributes which the Jains ascribe to the Supreme Being, the first is that he is "one" and "indivisible"; an observation quite illuminating when we remember the intimate relationship which has existed between the Jains and the Law of Buddha.

2 "*Within it first arose desire, the primal germ of mind,*
   Which nothing with existence links, as sages searching find.
   The cord, transversely stretched, that spanned this universal frame,
   Was it beneath? Was it above? Can any sage explain?"

— *"Progress of the Vedic religion towards abstract conceptions of the Deity"*. J. MUIR

3 "Free from self, free from life, free from personality, that highest perfect knowledge is always the same, and thus known with all good things. And why? Because, what was preached as good things, good things indeed, O Subhuti, they were preached by the Tathagata as no-things, and therefore they are called good things." — *The Vagrakkhedika*. MAX MÜLLER

"This condition which is named the unsurpassed, just, and enlightened (heart), consists in nothing more than the exclusion of all individual distinctions. A man who practices all the rules of virtuous conduct will forthwith attain this condition. But, Subhuti, when we speak of rules of virtuous conduct, Tathagata declares that these rules are after all no real and lasting rules; the term is but a mere name." — *Kin-Kong-King*. BEAL

they are merely termed 'Laws pertaining to goodness.'"¹

The Lord Buddha addressed Subhuti, saying: "If within this universe of universes, the seven treasures² were heaped together, forming as many great elevations as there are Sumerus, prince of mountains, and these treasures bestowed entirely in the exercise of charity; and if a disciple were to select a stanza of this Scripture, rigorously observe it, and diligently explain it to others, the merit³ thus obtained would so far exceed the former excellence, that it cannot be stated in terms of proportion, nor comprehended by

---

1 "The six *Paramita*: charity, morality, endurance, energy, contemplation, wisdom; comprehended under the term "laws pertaining unto goodness," merely constitute an open door by means of which disciples are ushered into the presence of truth. — *Chinese Annotation.*

2 Gold, silver, aquamarine, crystal, white coral, ruby and emerald.

3 "And whosoever in days when the good Law is abolished, abandons love for his own body and life, and proclaims day and night these good words; pre-eminent is his merit from this.

"He obtains a glorious and endless splendour who teaches even one word thereof; he will not miss one consonant nor the meaning who gives this Sutra to others. I therefore let those who are endowed with lofty ambitions, always hear this Law which causes transcendent merit; let them hear it and gladly welcome it, and lay it up in their minds, and continually worship the three jewels (the Buddha, the Law, and the assembly of monks) with faith." —*The Buddha-Karita.* COWELL

any analogy." [1]

The Lord Buddha addressed Subhuti, saying: "What think you? You disciples, do not affirm that the Lord Buddha reflects thus within himself. 'I bring salvation to every living being.' Subhuti, entertain no such delusive thought! And why? Because, in reality there are no living beings to whom the Lord Buddha can bring salvation.[2] If there were living beings to whom the Lord Buddha could bring salvation, the Lord

---

1 "I declare that his happiness and consequent merit would be incomparably greater than that of the other, so much so, that no number could express the excess of one over the other." — *Kin-Kong-King*. BEAL

2 As the primordial human mind is void and quiescent, so also is the wisdom of the Sutra full and overflowing, Therefore, hearing the text of this Sutra expounded, and meditating upon its truth, there are formed spontaneously within the minds of those living beings, all the essential elements of salvation. As these mature and develop into a Law of spiritual liberty, the Lord Buddha obviously relinquishes every duty consonant with the idea of a designated Saviour. — *Chinese Annotation*.

"What do you think then, O Subhuti, does a Tathagata think in this wise : beings have been delivered by me? You should not think so, And why? Because, there is no being that has been delivered by the Tathagata. And if there were a being, O Subhuti, that had been delivered by the Tathagata, then Tathagata would believe in a self, a being, a living being, and a person. And what is called a belief in self, O Subhuti, that is preached as a no-belief by the Tathagata. And this is learned by children and ignorant persons, and they who were preached as children and ignorant persons, O Subhuti, were preached as no-persons by the Tathagata, and therefore they are called children and ignorant persons."— *The Vagrakkhedika*. MAX MÜLLER

Buddha would necessarily assume the reality of such arbitrary concepts as an entity, a being, a living being, and a personality. Subhuti, what the Lord Buddha alluded to as an entity, is not in reality an entity; it is only understood to be an entity, and believed as such, by the common, uneducated people. Subhuti, what are ordinarily referred to as the 'common, uneducated people,' these the Lord Buddha declared to be not merely 'common, uneducated people.'" [1]

The Lord Buddha addressed Subhuti, saying: "Can the Lord Buddha be perceived by means of his thirty-two bodily distinctions?" [2] Subhuti replied, saying: "Even so, the Lord Buddha can be perceived by means of his thirty-two bodily distinctions."

The Lord Buddha, continuing, said unto Subhuti: "If by means of his thirty-two bodily

---

[1] "Difference there is in beings endowed with bodies, but amongst men this is not the case, the difference amongst men is nominal only." *Dhammapada.* MAX MÜLLER

"Worldly profit is fleeting and perishable, religious (holy) profit is eternal and inexhaustible; a man though a king is full of trouble, a common man who is holy, has everlasting rest."
— *Fo-Sho-Hing-Tsan-King.* BEAL

[2] "This probably refers to the auspicious signs discovered in Sakyamuni at his birth, which left open whether he would become a king or a Buddha." — *The Vagrakkhedika.* MÜLLER

distinctions it were possible to perceive the Lord Buddha, then the Lord Buddha would merely resemble one of the great wheel-turning kings."[1]

Subhuti thereupon addressed the Lord Buddha, saying: "Honoured of the Worlds! According as I am able to interpret the Lord Buddha's instruction, it is improbable that the Lord Buddha may be perceived by means of his thirty-two bodiless distinctions."

Thereupon, the "Honoured of the Worlds" delivered this sublime Gatha:

"I am not to be perceived by any visible form,
Nor sought after by means of any audible sound;

---

[1] "The portends troubled, till his dream-readers
Augured a prince of earthly dominance,
A Chakravartin, such as rise to rule
Once in a thousand years."

— *The Light of Asia.* ARNOLD

"A king who rules the world, and causes the wheel of doctrine everywhere to revolve. The great Asoka (King of Central India, who reigned near Patna, about 150-200 years after the demise of Buddha) was a 'wheel king.' The word is Chakravarti in Sanscrit, from Chakra 'wheel' the symbol of activity, whether of Buddha in preaching, or of kings like Asoka in ruling." — *Chinese Buddhism.* EDKINS

"Those of the Bikkhus who carry in their hearts the words of excellent knowledge that is immeasurable, who are free from bonds, whose fame and power and glory no man can weigh, who (in imitation of their master) keep the royal chariot wheel of the kingdom of righteousness rolling on, who have reached perfection in knowledge." — *Questions of King Melinda.* RHYS DAVIDS

*Whosoever walks in the way of iniquity,
Cannot perceive the blessedness of the Lord Buddha."* [1]

The Lord Buddha said unto Subhuti: "If you think thus within yourself, 'The Lord Buddha did not, by means of his perfect bodily distinctions, obtain supreme spiritual wisdom,' Subhuti, have no such deceptive thought! Or if you think thus within yourself, 'In obtaining supreme spiritual wisdom, the Lord Buddha declared the abrogation of every Law,' Subhuti, have no such delusive thought! And why? Because, those disciples who obtain supreme spiritual wisdom, neither affirm the abrogation of any Law, nor the destruction of any distinctive quality of phenomena." [2]

---

1 The following Gatha, translated by Max Müller, and concluding the twenty-sixth section of *The Vagrakkhedika*, is not incorporated in the Chinese text.
"*A Buddha is to be seen (known) from the Law;
For the Lords (Buddha) have the Law-Body;
And the nature of the Law cannot be understood,
Nor can it be made to be understood.*"

2 "What do you think then, O Subhuti, has the highest perfect knowledge been known by the Tathagata by the possession of signs? You should not think so, O Subhuti. And why? Because, the highest perfect knowledge wilt be known by the Tathagata through the possession of signs. Nor should anybody, O Subhuti, say to you that the destruction or annihilation of anything is proclaimed by those who have entered on the path of the Bodhisattva." — *The Vagrakkhedika.*
MAX MÜLLER

"Subhuti, if you should think thus, 'Tathagata, by means

The Lord Buddha addressed Subhuti, saying: "If an enlightened disciple, in the exercise of charity, bestowed as considerable an amount of the seven treasures as would fill worlds numerous as the sands of the Ganges; and if a disciple, realising that within the meaning and purport of the Law, there is no abstract individual existence,[1] perfects himself in the virtue of endurance, this latter discipline will have a cumulative merit, relatively greater than the other. And why?

---

of his personal distinctions has attained to the unsurpassable condition,' you would be wrong . . . But, Subhuti, do not come to such an opinion as this, viz., 'that what is called the unsurpassed, just and enlightened heart is nothing more than the mere neglect and destruction of all rules and conditions.' Think not so, for why? Because, The exhibition of this perfect and unsurpassed heart is not the consequence of disregarded and destroyed all rules, in the active discharge of duty." — *Kin-Kong-King*. BEAL

Concerning the phenomena of Law, if those were abrogated and discarded, where would the mind receive its guiding light, or the human spirit its power of discernment? To attempt a process of reasoning apart from such necessary postulates as the distinctive qualities of Law and phenomena, would prove to be as futile as an effort to cross a river without a raft, and would inevitably end in oblivion. — *Chinese Annotation.*

1 "And if a Bodhisattva acquired endurance in selfless and uncreated things, then he would enjoy a larger stock of merit, immeasurable and innumerable." — *The Vagrakkhedika* MAX MÜLLER

> "Nothing in this world is single,
> All things by a law divine
> In one another's being mingle." — SHELLEY

Because, enlightened disciples are entirely unaffected by considerations of 'reward and merit.'"

Subhuti thereupon enquired of the Lord Buddha, saying: "Honoured of the Worlds! In what respect are enlightened disciples unaffected by considerations of 'reward or merit?'" The lord Buddha replied, saying, "Enlightened disciples do not aspire, in a spirit of covetousness, to rewards commensurate with their merit; therefore, I declare that they are entirely unaffected by considerations of 'reward or merit.'"[1]

The Lord Buddha addressed Subhuti, saying: "If a disciple asserts that the Lord Buddha comes or goes, sits or reclines, obviously has not understood the meaning of my discourse. And why? Because, the idea 'Buddha' implies neither coming from anywhere, nor going anywhere, and hence

---

1 "Subhuti asked Buddha; World-honoured One! What is this you say, that Bodhisattvas cannot be said to appreciate reward? 'Subhuti, the reward which a Bodhisattva enjoys ought to be connected with no covetous desire; this is what I mean by non-appreciation of reward." — *Kin-Kong-King*. BEAL

This above passage, concluding the twenty-eighth section of *The Diamond Sutra*, not being incorporated in Max Müller's translation of *The Vagrakkhedika*, may be suggestive of a noteworthy interpolation in the Chinese text, or is it a possible lacuna in the Sanscrit M.S.S.?

the synonym 'Buddha!' "[1]

The Lord Buddha addressed Subhuti, saying: "If a good disciple, whether man or woman, were to take infinite worlds and 'reduce' them to minute particles of dust: what think you, would the aggregate of all

---

1 "And why? Because the word Tathagata means one who does not go to anywhere, and does not come from anywhere, and therefore he is called Tathagata (truly come), holy and enlightened." — *The Vagrakkhedika.* MAX MÜLLER

"That which is Tathagata has no where whence to come, and no where whither to go, and is therefore named Tathagata."— *Kin-Kong-King.* BEAL

"In the heavens above, we cannot discern a place whence he came, nor whither he may return, In his holy, immaculate and marvellously endowed body, were manifested plenary spiritual powers." — *Hua-Yen-Sutra.*

"Like drifting clouds, like the waning moon, like ships that sail the ocean, like shores that are washed away — these are symbolic of endless change. But the blessed Buddha, in his essential, absolute nature, is changeless and everlasting." — *Yuen-Chioh-Sutra*

"If the pool be of pure water, the shining moon is reflected upon its limped surface; and yet we cannot affirm that the moon really came from anywhere, or that it is actually in the pool. If the pool be disturbed and the dense mud raised, immediately the bright reflection becomes obscured; and yet we dare not affirm that the moon has really gone to anywhere, or that it has actually departed from the pool. It is entirely a question of the purity or impurity of the water, and has no reasonable affinity with theories concerning the existence or non-existence of the moon. So, also, with the true concept of Buddha; only those whose minds are immaculate in their pristine purity can ever release his transcendent blessedness." — *Chang-Shui* (a Chinese monk)

those particles of dust be great?"

Subhuti replied, saying: "Honoured of the Worlds! The aggregate of all those particles of dust would be exceedingly great. And why? Because, if all those were in reality 'minute particles of dust,' the Lord Buddha would not have declared them to be 'minute particles of dust.' And why? Because, the Lord Buddha, discoursing upon 'minute particles of dust,' declared that in reality those are not 'minute particles of dust,' they are merely termed 'minute particles of dust,' "[1]

---

1 "And why? Because the word Tathagata means one who does not go to anywhere, and does not come from anywhere, and therefore he is called Tathagata (truly come), holy and enlightened." — *The Vagrakkhedika.* MAX MÜLLER

"That which is Tathagata has no where whence to come, and no where whither to go, and is therefore named Tathagata."— *Kin-Kong-King.* BEAL

"In the heavens above, we cannot discern a place whence he came, nor whither he may return, In his holy, immaculate and marvellously endowed body, were manifested plenary spiritual powers." — *Hua-Yen-Sutra.*

"Like drifting clouds, like the waning moon, like ships that sail the ocean, like shores that are washed away — these are symbolic of endless change. But the blessed Buddha, in his essential, absolute nature, is changeless and everlasting." — *Yuen-Chioh-Sutra*

"If the pool be of pure water, the shining moon is reflected upon its limped surface; and yet we cannot affirm that the moon really came from anywhere, or that it is actually in the pool. If the pool be disturbed and the dense mud raised, immediately the bright reflection becomes obscured; and yet we dare not affirm that the moon has really gone to anywhere, or that it has actually

70 THE DIAMOND SUTRA

Subhuti continuing, addressed the Lord Buddha, saying: "Honoured of the Worlds! What Lord Buddha discoursed upon as 'infinite worlds,' these are not in reality 'infinite worlds.' And why? Because, if these were in reality 'infinite worlds,' there would of necessity be unity and eternity of matter. But the Lord Buddha, discoursing upon the 'unity and eternity of matter,' declared that there is neither 'unity' nor 'eternity of matter,' therefore it is merely termed 'unity and eternity of matter.'"

The Lord Buddha thereupon declared unto Subhuti,[1] "Belief in the unity or eternity

---

departed from the pool. It is entirely a question of the purity or impurity of the water, and has no reasonable affinity with theories concerning the existence or non-existence of the moon. So, also, with the true concept of Buddha; only those whose minds are immaculate in their pristine purity can ever release his transcendent blessedness." — *Chang-Shui* (a Chinese monk)

1 "Bhagavat said, and a belief in matter itself, O Subhuti, is inestimable and inexpressible; it is neither a thing nor a no-thing, and this is known by children and ignorant persons." — *The Vagrakkhedika*. MAX MÜLLER

"Annihilation of matter is inconceivable, but annihilation of all its forms and qualities is conceivable." — *The World as Idea and Will*. SCHOPENHAUER

If the worlds were real and permanent, they would always retain their original forms and primordial natures, and be subject neither to the influence of time, nor the Law of change. — *Chinese Annotation*.

"Subhuti, this characteristic of the 'one harmonious principle' is a thing which cannot be spoken of in words; it is only the

of matter is incomprehensible; and only common, worldly-minded people, for purely materialistic reasons, covet this hypothesis."[1]

The Lord Buddha addressed Subhuti, saying: "If a disciple affirmed that the Lord Buddha enunciated a belief[2] that the mind can

---

vain philosophy of the world, which has grasped the idea of explaining this."—
Kin-Kong-King. BEAL

1 This noteworthy statement seems to militate against some opinions expressed in the West regarding the Buddhist theory of "matter." According to our Chinese text, it does not appear that Sakyamuni categorically denied the "presence" or "existence" of matter in the universe, but endeavoured rather to indicate the diversified and evanescent nature of its "forms" and "qualities." Many devout Buddhists regard even the smallest particle of dust as containing a mysterious and elusive element — probably what those in the West are disposed to term a "spiritual element," or "principle of life" — and these are not unreasonably regarded as being altogether inscrutable, and therefore "incomprehensible."
— *Chinese Annotation.*

2 "Because, O Subhuti, if a man were to say that belief in self, belief in a being, belief in life, belief in personality, had been preached by the Tathagata, would he be speaking truly? Subhuti said, not indeed, Bhagavat, he would not be speaking truly. And why? Because, what was preached by the Tathagata as a belief in self, that was preached as a no-belief, therefore it is called belief in self." — *The Vagrakkhedika.* MAX MÜLLER

In these words are exemplified another profound aspect of Buddhist doctrine. Apart from interesting questions concerning the existence of an entity, a being, a living being, or a personality, another problem seems to arise concerning our ability to entirely perceive or "comprehend" those admitted abstract ideas. If we interpret aright the Buddhist doctrine, there are variously compounded within those abstract ideas, so many elusive spiritual elements, that the human mind is incapable of resolving

comprehend the idea of an entity, a being, a living being, or a personality; what think you, Subhuti, would that disciple be interpreting aright the meaning of my discourse?" Subhuti replied, saying, "Honoured of the Worlds! That disciple would not be interpreting aright the meaning of the Lord Buddha's discourse. And Why? Because, Honoured of the Worlds! Discoursing upon comprehending such ideas as an entity, a being, a living being, and a personality, it was declared that these are entirely unreal and elusive, and therefore they are merely termed an entity, a being, a living being, and a personality."

The Lord Buddha thereafter addressed Subhuti, saying:[1] "Those who aspire to the

---

them by any process of reasoning. In short; an entity, a being, a living being, or a personality, represents, to the Buddhist mind, much more than it attempts to express in terms of philosophy. — *Chinese Annotation.*

1 "Thus then, O Subhuti, are all things to be perceived, to be looked upon, and believed by one who has entered upon the path of the Bodhisattvas. And in this wise are they to be perceived, to be looked upon, and believed, neither in the idea of a thing, nor of a no-thing? And why? Because, the idea of a thing, the idea of a thing indeed, has been preached by the Tathagata as the no-idea of a thing." — *The Vagrakkhedika.* MAX MÜLLER

"Subhuti, the persons who aspire to the perfectly enlightened heart, ought to know accordingly that this is true with respect to all things, and thus prevent the exhibition of any characteristics on any point whatever. Subhuti, these very characteristics of which we speak are after all no characteristics, but a mere name."

attainment of supreme spiritual wisdom, ought thus to know, believe in and interpret phenomena. They ought to eliminate from their minds every tangible evidence of every visible object. Subhuti, concerning 'visible objects,' the Lord Buddha declared that these are not really 'visible objects,' they are merely termed 'visible objects.'"

The Lord Buddha addressed Subhuti, saying: "If a disciple, having immeasurable spheres filled with the seven treasures,[1] bestowed these in the exercise of charity; and if a disciple, whether man or woman, having aspired to supreme spiritual wisdom, selected from this Scripture a stanza comprising four lines, then rigorously observes it, studies it, and diligently explains it to others, the cumulative merit of such a disciple would be relatively greater than the other.

"In what attitude of mind should it be diligently explained to others?[2] Not assuming

---

— *Kin-Kong-King.* BEAL

1 Gold, silver, aquamarine, crystal, white coral, ruby and emerald.

2 "The wise man, the teacher, who wishes to expound this Sutra, must absolutely renounce falsehood, pride, calumny, and envy... He is always sincere, mild, forbearing... he must feel affection for all beings who are striving for enlightenment... They are greatly perverted in their minds, those beings who do not hear, nor perceive... the mystery of the Tathagata.

the permanency or the reality of earthly phenomena, but in the conscious blessedness of a mind at rest,[1] And why? Because, the phenomena of life may be likened to a dream, a phantom, a bubble,[2] a shadow, the glistening dew, or lightning flash, and thus they ought to be contemplated."

Nevertheless will I, who have attained this supreme, perfect knowledge, powerfully bend to it the mind of every one (Burnouf: *par la force de mess facultès surnaturelles*), whatever may be the position he occupies, and bring about that he accepts, understands, and arrives at full ripeness." — *Saddharma-Pundarika*. KERN

1 "By contemplation are obtained those conditions through which is eventually gained that supreme calm, undecaying, immortal state, which is so hard to be reached." — *The Buddha-Karita*. COWELL

"And in what way can the disciple proclaim them generally? Simply be relying on no conditions or distinctions whatever; thus he will act without agitation or excitement. Wherefore the conclusion is this — that all things which admit of definition are as a dream, a phantom, a bubble, a shadow, as the dew and lightning flash. They ought to be regarded thus." — *Kin-Kong-King*. BEAL

"And how should he explain it? As in the sky: stars, darkness, a lamp, a phantom, dew, a bubble, a dream, a flash of lightning, and a cloud — thus should we look upon the world (all that was made)." — *The Vagrakkhedika*. MAX MÜLLER

2 "Fa-Hien stayed at the dragon Vihara till after the summer retreat, and then, travelling to the south-east for seven Yojanas, he arrived at the city of Kanyakubja, lying along the Ganges . . . At a distance from the city of six of seven *le*, on the west, on the northern bank of the Ganges, is a place where Buddha preached the Law to his disciples. It has been handed down that the subjects of his discourse were such as 'The bitterness and vanity (of life), as impermanent and uncertain,' and that 'The body is as a "bubble" or foam on the water.' " — *Travels of Fa-Hien*. LEGGE

THE DIAMOND SUTRA

When the Lord Buddha concluded his enunciation of the Scripture,[1] the venerable Subhuti, the monks,[2] nuns, lay-bretheren and sisters, all mortals and the whole realm of spiritual beings, rejoiced exceedingly, and consecrated to its practice, they received it and departed.

---

1 "Thus spake the Bhagavad enraptured; the elder Subhuti, and the friars, nuns, the faithful lay men and women, and the Bodhisattvas also, and the whole world of gods, men, evil spirits and fairies, praised the preaching of the Bhagavat." — *The Vagrakkhedika.* MAX MÜLLER

2 "The vow of 'obedience' was never taken by the monks and nuns, and in this it may be noted a fundamental difference between the Sangha and monastic orders in the West. Mental culture, not mental death, was the aim set before the Buddhist ascetic by the founder of his faith." — *Buddhism.* RHYS DAVIDS

INDEX

Alexandria 14
Alms-bowl 3, 4
Almsgiving 2, 9, 10
Anagami 21
Ananda ....xxi, 8
Anepidu 35
Anniversaries 45, 124
Anta-Kalpas 28
Anuradhapura 34
Anurogrammum 34
Apatti 19
Aranyaka 24
Arhat...................... 21, 22, 23, 27, 55
Ari-Hat 22
Arjuna................................ xxii, 39
Arnold, Sir Edwin .. xix, xxvi, xxxi, 7, 12, 14, 23, etc.
Arya 21, 22
Aryagiti 18
Arya-Marga 22
Ascetic (-ism)............... xxix, 10, 14, 24, 39, 49
Asiatic........................... xii, xiii, xxvi
Asoka ....xvi, 66
Asurus................................... 29
Asvaghocha..............................xiv, 6
Atman.................................... 34
Atoms 32, 33, 71
Attavada 8
Awakening of Faith ....xiv, 6
Bacche, The 13
Bana 30, 35
Beal, Samuel ..... ix, x, xii, xiii, xv, xxv, 1, 5, 10, etc.
Benares 1
Benefactions 2
Bhagavad-Gita ....xix, xxix, xxxi, 5, 23
Bhagavat............... 16, 25, 31, 72, 73, 77
Bhoga-Deha 58
Bikkhus................................... 66
Bikshu.................................... 5
Bikshuni 5
Bodhi 4, 43, 44

Bodhisattva......xii, xxi, 4, 5, 25, 40, 48, 52, 53, etc.
Bodily distinctions..........xxiv, 33, 34, 65, 66, 67
Bo-Tree.................................... 49
Brahman .... xxvi, 1, 11, 48, 58, etc.
Brahmanas 1
Brahmanical 58
Brahmanism 11
Buddha.................... xi, xii, xiii, xxvi, etc.
Buddhas, numerous .... 4, 5, 7, 9, 10, 11, 13, 17, etc.
Buddha-Karita 60, 63, 76
Buddhaphalam 22
Buddhaship 5, 10, 22. 25,
Buddhic .... xiv, xvii, 19, 42, 43, 55, 57, etc.
Buddhism .... xii, xvi, (etc), 1, 2, etc.
Burnouf.................................... 76
Calingapatah 38
Ceremonies, religious (efficacy of) ....xix, 8, 62
Ceylon............................. 4, 34, 42, 56
Ceylon Friend 42
Chakra 66
Chakravartin 66
Chang-Ming .... x, 13
Chang-Shui................................ 70
Chiliocosm................................ 33
China .... xi, xii, xiii, 4, 13, etc.
Chinese Buddhism .... 18, 19, 21, 24, 25, etc.
Chioh-Hsien 7
Christ 12, 16, 26, 44, 51
Christian .... xvii, xxvii, 16, 49, 51
Circars..................................... 38
Clouds........................ xviii, xxi, xxv, 69
Coral 17, 45, 57, 63, 75
Carnelian 17, 28, 45, 57, 63, 75
Cowell, E. B.......................... 60, 63, 76
Creed 32,33
Cross (over, etc) 7, 30, 43, 63
Crystal 17, 28, 45, 57, 63, 75
Danataka Aranyaka 24
Dapankara 24
Davids, T. W. Rhys .... xvi, xix, xxvii, xxx, etc.

INDEX

Davis, Sir John Francis. 13
Delusions, the three primary. 8
Dewa-Loka 20
Devas 21
Dhamma . . . . xvi, 18 23, 29, 35
Dhammo . . . . .xvi, 54
Dharma. . . . . xv, xvi, xxvii, xix, 9, 21, etc.
Dharma Aranyaka 24
Dharma-Kaya. 58
Dharmasala. 45
Dharmma . . . . .xvi, 18, 54
Diamond Sutra, The. . . . . ix, xi, xii, xiii etc.
Dipankara Buddha. 35, 46, 49, 50
Djatakas 2
Dubois, the Abbé 62
Eastern Monachism . xvi, 3, 10, 14, 18, 20, 23, 24, etc.
Edkins, Joseph . . . . xi, xvi, 2, 5, 6, 26, 48, 52, etc.
Egypt. . . . . .xxvi, 14
Eitel. . . . . .xii, xvi, xxii, 1, 2, 4, 5, etc.
Elburz 26
Eleusis 45
Enlightenment of Ananda . . . . .xxi, 8
Enlightenment of the Buddha 48-49
Euripides. 13
Europe. . . . . .vi, x, 14
Fa-Hien 1, 45, 76
Fah . . . . .xvi, 9, 41
Fah-Ai. 9
Fah-Luen. 9
Fah-Men 9
Fah-Ming 9
Fah-Pao 9
Fah-Shen . . . . xxiv, 11
Fah-Wang 9
Fah-Yen 54
Fairies 77
Faith . . . . vi, xii. xiv, xxviii, xxix, 2, 4, 5, etc.
Fausboll 16, 19, 45
Fei-Fuh-Fah 19
Fo-Sho-Hing-Tsan-King 65

INDEX

Form, emptiness of 55-56
Fox 47
Fuh 12
Gandhara 4
Ganges 1, 27, 28, 34, 42, 55, 68, 76
Gatha .... xxiv, 18, 67
Gautama 44, 48, 56
German .... xiii, 14
Girdle 2
Glass 17, 28, 45, 57, 63, 75
God 13, 14
Gods 29, 77
Gogerly, Rev. D. J. 42
Gold 13, 17, 28, 45, 57, 63, 75
Gondophares 6
Gotama 35
Greek .... xvi, 14
Gungas 28
Happiness 18, 19, 58, 64
Hardy, Spence .... xvi, xxix, 3, 10, 14, 18, 20, etc.
Heresy .... xix, 8, 30
Hero 33
Hindu 24, 44
Hindu Manners, Customs, and Ceremonies 62
Hinduism 46
Hiuen-Tsang .... xi, 1, 2, 34, 36, 45
Ho-Ru-To-Lo-San-Mao-San-Pu-Ti 5
Ho-Tan-Ju-Lai 44
Hua-Yen-Sutra 70
Hunter, Sir William 37
Icicles 60
Idea and Will, The World as 32, 72
Immortality 7, 29
Immortals 1
India .... xi, xvi, xxvi, 5, 14, 37, etc.
Indian Empire, The 37
Indo-Scythic 6
I-Wu-Wei-Fah 17
Jains 62
Jayendra 36

INDEX

Jesus 12, 26, 44
Jeta 1, 2, 3
Jewels 9, 63
Kalinga 38
Kaliradja 39
Kalpa 4, 28, 30
Kanyakubja 76
Karma .... xxvii, xxviii
Karmic manifestation..................... 45-46
Kashaya 34
Kasina...................................... 24
Kasmir 45
Kern, H. 37, 40, 76
Khaloupas Waddhaktinka 3
Kin-Kong-King......... xv, xxv, 1, 5, 10, 17, 28, etc.
Kingdoms 25, 26, 45, 53
Kos'ala 38
Kshanti 39
Kshantivadin 40
Lao-Tsz............................. ix, xxvii, 19
Lay-bretheren.............................. 77
Legge...................................... 45, 76
Light of Asia, The .. xiv, xxviii, xxix, xxxi, 7, 12, etc.
Lotus of the Good Law..................... xi, 44
Love.............. xxviii, xxx, 9, 37, 49, 50, 51, 63
Ma-Ming .... xiv, 6
Madhyades'a 4
Mahasattvas 5
Mahayana......................... xi, xxi, 43
Mahayana doctrine......................... xx
Mantras..................................... 1
Matanga 24
Materialist............................... 32, 73
Maya 33, 39
Meditate, meditation 18. 22. 24. 37. 47
Memoires sur-les Contrées Occidentalees 2
Mencius ix
Mendicant 2, 3, 5
Metamorphosis .... xix, 2
Mieh-Tu 7

Milinda 3, 20, 79
Milton 49
Mo-Ho-Sa 5
Mo-Wei-Sutra 53
Muir, J. .... xxvi, 62
Müller, Max ix, x, xi, xiii, xv, xvi, xxx, 17, 19, 21, etc.
Murray, Gilbert 13
Myak...................................... 5
Nairanjara 49
Narakas 30
Needle.................................... 2
Nibbana 16
Nihilism .... xi, 48
Nimitta 24
Nirmanakaya 11
Nirvana .... xiii, xiv, xix, 31, 1, 5, 6, 7, 9, 11, etc.
Non-individuality....................... xxx, 53
Nuttara 5
Oedipus Coloneus 45
Padumas 32
Pali .... xvi, 56
Paramita .... xi, xii, 4, 6, 9, 38, 39, 63
Patna.................................... 66
Path .... xiii, xiv, 8, 10, 12, 19, 20, 22, 29, 38, etc
Paul, the Apostle 16, 44
Pearls..................... 17, 28, 45, 57, 63, 75
Persia 4
Pilgrims 1, 45
Po-Ro-Po-Lo-Mi 6
Prajna-Paramita .... xii, 4, 6, 38
Prakrita................................. 39
Prasenajit 1
Priests 3, 36, 45
Ptolemy................................. 35
Puh-Seng 22
Pundarikas 32
Pu-sa..................................... 4
Questions of King Milinda 3, 20, 79
Raft .... xix, xxviii, 16, 20, 67
Rahat 14

INDEX

Rahatship 23
Ran-Teng-Fuh 25
Razor 2
Reality, the true nature of 37-42, 75-76
Rebirth .... xxvi, xxviii, xxix, 20, 21
Regents 26
Reincarnation .... xxix, xxx
Religious rites and ceremonies, efficacy of 8
Relation des Royaumes 3
Remusat 3
Ren 29
Righteousness .... xvi, xvii, xvii, xxx, 11, 66, 79
Rishi 40
Rites and ceremonies, efficacy of .... xix, 8, 62
Robe 2, 3, 34
Saddharma-Pundarika 40, 76
Sagara 4
Sakkayaditthi 8
Sakridagami 20
Sakyamuni   xii, xv, xvii, xviii, xix, xxi, xxiv, xxv, xxvi, etc.
Salvation 7, 43, 55, 64, 65
Samadhi 24
Sambhoga-Kaya 58
Sambodhi .... xv, 5
Samma-Sambuddha 56
Sangha 29
San-Pao 11
Sanscrit ..... ix, xiii, xiv, xv, xvi, xvii, xix, 1, 3, 5, etc.
Sarvanikchepa 28
Sarwajnan-Wahanse........................ 56
Sasa 30
Sattva 4
Saviour .... xxx, 2, 64
Schelling, Friedrich 14
Schopenhauer, Arthur..................... 32, 72
Scripture ...... xxiv, 1, 6, 12, 13, 14, 18, 19, 29, etc.
Scrota 19
Scrotapatti 19, 20
Seh-Shen 11

INDEX

Selfhood 27
Seven treasures........... xvi, 17, 28, 56, 62, 68, 75
Sewet 35
Shah-Tseh 22
Shelley 69
Shen-Ming 34
Shore .... xviii, xxv, 6, 18, 30, 31, 43, 70
Shravasti 1, 3, 4
Siao-Fah 44
Signs 33, 59. 65, 67, 68
Silver 13, 17, 28, 45, 57, 63, 75
Senagalese 16, 55
Siddhārtha 48
Siva 11
Sivaism 11
Sophocles 45
Spawn 6
Spirits 14, 29, 49, 58, 77
Spiritualist 32
Sramana 24
S'ruti 1
Sthula 58
Subhuti .... xlii, xviii, xix, 4, 5, 6, 8, etc.
Sumeru 26, 27, 40
Sutana 2
Sutra .... ix, xii, xiii, xiv, xv, xvi, xvii, etc.
Sutta-Nipata 16, 45
Swastika 33
Syria ....xxvi, 14
Sz-ti 22
Ta-Chen-Che 43
Talents............................ 36, 43, 55
Tang (dynasty) 52
Ta-Pi-Ku 2
Tathagata xi, xxv, 12, 17, 19, 25, 27, 32, 33, 38, 42, etc.
Teacher .... xxx, 2, 18, 30, 42, 49
Temples 34
Tennyson 16
Thomson, J. Cockburn 5, 23, 48
Ti-Ching 8

INDEX

Tien 29
Tien-Kong 20
Ting-Kwang-Fuh 25
Topes.................................... 45
Treasures............... xvi, 17, 28, 56, 62, 68, 75
Trimurti 11
Triratna 11
Truth   xiii, xiv, xvi, xvii, xviii, xxvi, 18, 19, 22, 28, 42, 43, etc.
Tuchita 4
Twan-Tsi-Sin-Yao 52
Upadanas 8
Vagrakkhedika, The xi, xx, 19, 21, 25, 27, 30 , 31, etc.
Vais'ali 4
Vedas 1
Vedic .... xxvi, 62
Vice 2
Vihara 76
Virtue ..... xii, xx, xxx, 1, 2, 9, 10, 13, 37, 39, 46, 68
Vows 2, 5, 13, 24, 38
Waddhaktinka 3
Waterfall 60
Water-strainer 2
West 73, 76, 77
Wiharas 34
Williams, Sir Monier 32, 43, 46, 58
Wisdom .... ix, xii
Wou-Wei 17
Wu-Wei, Fah 17, 19
Yen-Ping 61
Yogi 14
Yojanas 76
Yuen-Chioh Sutra .... xxv, 70

"As when men, travelling, feel a glorious perfume sweet
Pervading all, and gladdening them, infer at once,
'Surely 'tis giant forest trees are flowering now!'
And so, conscious of this perfume sweet, of righteousness,
That now pervades both earth and heavens, they may infer:
'A Buddha, infinitely great, must once have lived!'"

— *The Questions of King Milinda*, translated by T. W. Rhys Davids

www.ingramcontent.com/pod-product-compliance
Lightning Source LLC
Chambersburg PA
CBHW040244010526
44107CB00065B/2875